NEWB~~RI~~ **~~L~~INKS**
Guided Reading Th~~rough~~ Social Studies

Teacher's Guide

Fluent Level

Brenda Parkes

Newbridge Discovery Links:
Guided Reading Through Social Studies
Teacher's Guide—Fluent Level
ISBN: 1-58273-560-3

Written by Brenda Parkes
Edited and designed by Kirchoff/Wohlberg, Inc.

Newbridge Educational Publishing
11 East 26th Street, New York, NY 10010
www.newbridgeonline.com

10 9 8 7 6 5 4

Table of Contents

Dr. Brenda Parkes

Dr. Brenda Parkes is a well-known Australian educator and author who conducts keynote presentations, workshops, and seminars in the United States, Canada, Britain, and Australia. Brenda trained as an early childhood teacher in New Zealand and taught there for some years before moving to Australia. Until recently she was a senior lecturer in Literacy Education at Griffith University.

Brenda also works with school districts in the United States and Australia as an on-site literacy consultant for early childhood literacy programs. Her work keeps her in frequent contact with teachers and children in early childhood settings.

Brenda has written many books for shared and guided reading, including her first non-fiction guided reading program for Newbridge, *Discovery Links Science*. Her most recent professional book, *Read It Again,* is published by Stenhouse Publishers.

Introduction

What Is Guided Reading?

Guided reading involves supporting a small group of students thinking, talking, and reading purposefully through a new text with guidance from the teacher. Grouping is dynamic and includes children who are at a similar developmental level and share needs and behaviors at a particular time.

The purpose of guided reading is to help children develop effective skills and strategies that they can use flexibly and appropriately to:

- comprehend what they read
- figure out unknown words
- read and understand new sentence structures

Through ongoing observation and assesment, the teacher chooses books at increasing levels of challenge to:

- support children to use what they already know
- challenge children to learn and apply new skills and strategies

Fluent Readers

Fluent readers are able to use a variety of different resources and information in an integrated way. They focus mainly on meaning, and use subject matter and the organization of the text to maintain their reading in a fluent, phrased way.

Although there will be variations among individuals depending on their experiences and capabilities, fluent readers generally:

- are able to maintain meaning and momentum while solving unfamiliar words
- carry meaning over longer, more complex texts
- read silently for longer periods of time
- use letter clusters and syllables more than single letters to confirm
- use pictures and other visuals to confirm and extend the meaning of the written language
- move between using word analysis and meaning to solve unfamiliar words
- take increasing responsibility for their own reading
- respond to texts through a variety of writing forms, visuals, and graphic organizers

Why Non-Fiction Guided Reading?

Research shows that 80% of the reading and writing we do every day is non-fiction. Non-fiction reading is also featured in all national testing. In this "age of information," it is vital that students understand how to gather, interpret, and communicate information. This process requires an understanding of:

- the different ways information can be read and communicated (for example, through photographs, diagrams, maps, charts, tables, and other forms of visual depictions)
- the specialized language and language structures used in non-fiction texts
- the way non-fiction is organized to highlight information
- the selective way non-fiction is read according to the reader's purpose

Why a Social Studies Focus?

It is the goal of *Discovery Links* to help children develop a sense of where they are in time, in space, and in culture— to have a sense of personal and social identity.

Social studies engages children in the study of history, geography, economics, government, and civics. As children are beginning to understand themselves as individuals and in relation to others, social studies concepts encourage them to examine issues and raise questions, such as:

- How are we the same as and different from those who have come before us?
- What do all people have in common?
- Which individuals and groups have contributed to our development?
- What are our responsibilities to ourselves, to others, and to society?
- What are our greatest achievements as a nation?
- Who are we as a nation, and what are our values and traditions?
- What is our place in the world?
- How do we celebrate diversity and unity?
- What will we be like in the future? How will we protect our planet and its people?

The study of social studies helps children understand their roots, see their connections to the past, recognize the commonality of people across time and place, appreciate the balance of rights and responsibilities in an open society, and develop the habits of research, problem solving, and reasoned decision making.

Language Arts Standards

The *Discovery Links* books help children achieve the Language Arts Standards (the excerpts listed below have been extracted from the Compendium of Standards and Benchmarks for K–12 Education). These standards help ensure that the student:

- comprehends the main idea of simple expository information

- recognizes characteristic sounds and rhythms of language

- demonstrates a basic familiarity with selected non-fiction

- makes simple inferences regarding, "What will happen next…?"

- demonstrates competence in speaking and listening as tools for learning

- understands that reading is a way of gaining information about the world

- creates mental pictures for concrete information he or she has read

- uses picture clues and picture captions as aids to comprehension

- writes compositions that make effective use of very general, frequently used words to convey basic ideas

- demonstrates competence in the general skills and strategies of the writing process

24 Titles for Fluent Readers

Discovery Links books have been carefully developed to facilitate guided reading for fluent readers. Each title follows a specific, non-fiction structural format, such as:

- descriptive
- sequence
- cause and effect
- problem/solution
- compare/contrast

In *Reading Maps*, for example, children will find a compare/contrast structure:

A Neighborhood

This is a photograph of houses in a neighborhood. The photo was taken by a person in a helicopter. This kind of photo is called a bird's-eye view. 6 It's how a bird might see the houses.

This is a map of the same houses in the same neighborhood. Most maps show a bird's-eye view. They show what a place looks like from above. 7

In *Taking Care of Trees*, children will experience a cause-and-effect structure:

How Trees Help Us

These students are planting new trees along a busy street. The new trees will help keep the air fresh and clean.

These workers are planting trees by a river. A tree's roots help keep soil from washing away when a river floods.

4

5

The title *Making Choices* illustrates a problem/solution structure:

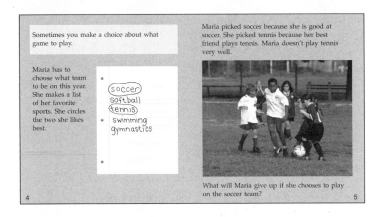

Sometimes you make a choice about what game to play.

Maria has to choose what team to be on this year. She makes a list of her favorite sports. She circles the two she likes best.

- soccer
  softball
  tennis
- swimming
  gymnastics

Maria picked soccer because she is good at soccer. She picked tennis because her best friend plays tennis. Maria doesn't play tennis very well.

What will Maria give up if she chooses to play on the soccer team?

4   5

In *National Parks*, children encounter a descriptive structure:

Glacier National Park is in Montana. The park is named for its **glaciers**. Glaciers are frozen rivers of ice. A glacier forms at the top of a mountain and then moves slowly down it.

6

Visitors to this park can hike along trails and see the lakes, mountains, and other landforms created by glaciers a long time ago.

7

Yellowstone National Park is in three states: Wyoming, Idaho, and Montana. Old Faithful is in the park. It is a **geyser** that shoots hot water out of the ground about every 76 minutes.

10

Yellowstone National Park is home to many different animals, including this **cougar**. Cougars are great climbers and jumpers and can run up to 35 miles an hour.

11

Non-Fiction Features of Discovery Links Guided Reading Books

The books in this program have been designed to encourage and support children's use of the many features found in informational books. These features include:

• the organizational patterns and layout features that provide access to information, such as contents pages, indexes, and headings

• the specialized language and language structures of informational texts

• the use of photographs, charts, diagrams, tables, drawings, and other forms of visual literacy

Children will have many opportunities to use these features in reading and as powerful models for writing on topics relating to social studies.

All books are illustrated with superb photographs that support and extend the written language.

Cinco de Mayo

Cinco de Mayo is our special celebration. We celebrate our Mexican heritage with dancing and parades.

6

People use roads to travel from place to place. Animals have to get from place to place, too. This sign warns drivers that deer cross the road around here.

14

A New Hive

This swarm of buzzing bees and their queen are searching for the best place to build a new hive.

2

This gymnastics team won gold medals. They are from the United States.

15

The Paper Mill

The next step is making the chips into pulp. The wood chips are boiled in a giant tub with bleach, water, and chemicals. When the wood chips become wet and soggy, they are called wood pulp.

At the paper mill, the logs are put into a big drum. The drum spins around to take off the bark. Bark is too tough to make into paper. A machine grinds the logs into wood chips.

6

7

Deep in the ground, the Pueblo people built a room called a kiva. This is where the Pueblo people met. Often they built a fire in the center of the room.

Today, the Pueblo people still use kivas as a place to meet and spend time together.

8

9

Plymouth Today

Today, we can learn what life was like for the Pilgrims by visiting Plymouth Plantation. It is a small village like the one the Pilgrims built. There people show visitors how the Pilgrims lived.

10

11

Contents pages are supported by pictograms.

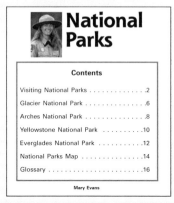

National Parks

Contents

Mary Evans

Indexes introduce children to the concept of looking up topics.

Index

Maps provide young readers with clear examples of this feature of informational texts.

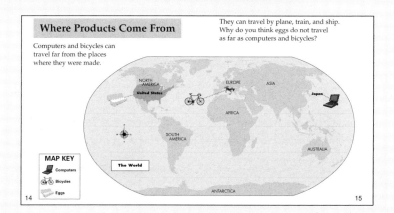

Charts model ways of presenting information through graphic organizers.

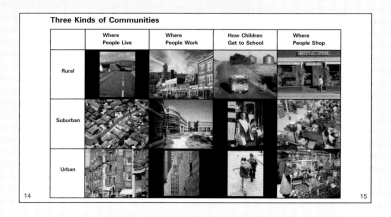

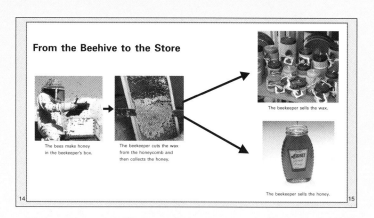

From the Beehive to the Store

The bees make honey in the beekeeper's box.

The beekeeper cuts the wax from the honeycomb and then collects the honey.

The beekeeper sells the wax.

The beekeeper sells the honey.

14

15

Chicago Time Line

1833 · THE CITY GROWS
By 1833, the city of Chicago begins to grow as people build houses and other buildings around Fort Dearborn.

1850s · LUMBER CENTER
By the 1850s, Chicago was becoming one of the largest lumber centers in the world. Logs were sent to factories in Chicago to be made into boards.

1871 · FIRE!
In 1871, there was a huge fire in Chicago. It burned for 24 hours, destroying much of the city.

1885 · THE FIRST SKYSCRAPER
The world's first skyscraper was built in Chicago in 1885. It was only nine stories high.

TODAY · SEARS TOWER
Today, you can find the tallest building in the United States in Chicago. It is called the Sears Tower, and it is 110 stories high.

16

Our Neighbors: Canada and Mexico

CANADA

Capital:	Ottawa
Official Languages:	English and French
Population:	29,123,194 (as of 1998)
Highest Point:	Mount Logan (19,524 feet)
Geography:	3,849,674 square miles. Canada is the largest country in North America.

MEXICO

Capital:	Mexico City
Official Language:	Spanish
Population:	97,563,374 (as of 1998). Mexico has the second largest population in North America.
Highest Point:	Orizaba Mountain (18,701 feet)
Geography:	758,136 square miles

16

How Children Vote

These children are going to **vote**. They are going to vote on where the class should go on their field trip. Each child in the class will vote for one place. Each child's vote will be counted.

2

Our Field Trip		
Zoo	🐘	llll
Children's Museum	🦕	llll
Aquarium	🐬	llll lll

This chart shows how the children voted. Votes were counted by making **tally marks**. Each child voted for one place. Each vote got a mark like this: l.

This shows four votes: llll. This shows five votes: llll.

Most of the **voters** chose the aquarium.

3

Overview of Teacher's Notes

The teacher's notes for *Discovery Links* provide:

• important features built into each book that support guided reading

• a suggested sequence for talking, thinking, and reading through the book the first time

• suggestions for observing and prompting independent oral reading

• ideas for discussing the reading process and book content

These notes are intended as a guide to be used flexibly and appropriately according to the students' individual experiences, knowledge, and needs. The ultimate goal is to support children to predict, sample, confirm, and self-monitor by integrating semantic, syntactic, and graphophonic information to break through to meaning at the first reading.

• In addition, there are suggestions for related reading, writing, and social studies activities and projects.

• A comprehensive bibliography of fiction and non-fiction books that relate to each title can be found on pages 100–105.

Using the Teacher's Notes

The teacher's notes for each of the 24 titles follow a consistent format. The following features are included for each title:

Benchmarks and Standards
Correlation to the National Council of Social Studies (NCSS), the National Geography Standards, K-4, and the Compendium of Standards and Benchmarks for K-12 Education.

Supports
In this section you will find a list of features from the book that support the reader, such as consistent placement of print, repetitive language, and photo/text match. These assist the student in maintaining the flow of meaning.

Challenges
This bulleted list displays the features of the book that may challenge the reader, such as unfamiliar vocabulary, a change in the repetitive language pattern, or a particular non-fiction feature. The unfamiliar features may provide some challenge, requiring the teacher to be observant of the way the student works to predict and confirm the text and its message. The teacher will then be able to identify skills and strategies requiring instruction and focused practice.

Using the Teacher's Notes (continued)

The lists headed "Supports" and "Challenges" should not be considered exclusive or arbitrary. What proves to be a support for one student may be a challenge for another. Prior to the lesson, the teacher will be able to reflect on the features which are likely to cause some difficulty, and then be mindful of these as the lesson progresses. The supports and challenges include graphophonic, syntactic, and semantic features of text as well as those relating to photo support, layout, and concepts.

Text features

This analysis highlights structure, organization, visual text, and language. Although a number of features may appear in each book, only focus on those that have become important during the reading. The items listed under "Text Features" will enable the teacher to identify opportunities to observe or support the students applying skills and strategies appropriate for their stage in reading development. These features will also provide a focus for guidance and practice in writing.

Introducing the text

The suggestions in this section link the reader's own experiences, knowledge, and understanding with the concept explored in the text. The focus is on meaning. The suggestions relate directly to each book. However, if the concept is outside the experience of an individual or the group, the discussion may need to begin with a concrete experience or hands-on exploration.

Using the Teacher's Notes (continued)

The introduction to a non-fiction book should remind the students of their roles as readers in accessing and processing information, and of their repertoire of knowledge, strategies, and skills to do that. Suggestions in this section will help teachers decide how to:

- use the title and book-cover information to identify the topic and its probable treatment
- establish what is already known about the topic
- consider how to access further information or concepts
- remind students that they can learn about other people and their lives as well as their own
- set a purpose for the reading

This section of the lesson should engender enthusiasm for the book and an expectation within each student that the book can help him or her learn more about the topic and about reading. It should also help the teacher confirm which features listed in the earlier sections of the "Teacher's Notes" will probably provide a focus for the amount and nature of instruction, support, or monitoring. For example, if the introductory discussion indicates that the topic or concept may not be within a student's real or vicarious experience, more time will need to be spent linking the known to the unknown.

Using the Teacher's Notes (continued)

The first reading

These notes provide suggested questions and prompts to help ensure that students gain and maintain meaning on the first reading. The questions and prompts reflect the intent of the supports and challenges listed in the earlier sections and link these to the section entitled "Text Features." They are based on the premise that it is the reader's (i.e., in guided reading, the student's) responsibility to apply skills and strategies to break through to understanding on the first reading. Your role is to provide only as much support as necessary for the student to decode and process the text. Therefore, the suggestions provided in this section will need to be adapted according to the competencies the students display at the time of the reading. The suggestions aim to ensure that students develop the habit of confirming predictions and, where necessary, employing strategies to self-correct in order to maintain accurate and fluent reading. *The extent to which teachers use these suggestions depends on the needs of each particular group.*

To read effectively, *all* readers draw from and integrate various kinds of information to create meaning from text. This involves attending and sampling, predicting, checking and confirming, and self-correcting. The instructional learning context of guided reading provides children with the opportunity to learn and practice these strategies:

attending and sampling: scanning the text for known words, familiar concepts, and familiar patterns, such as *letter clusters* and *word endings*.

predicting: searching for clues to meaning based on background experiences and knowledge of written and oral language.

checking and confirming: knowing their predicting makes sense and sounds and looks right.

The information children draw on to reconstruct meaning comes from language-based sources of information, or cues. *Semantic* information relates to the meaning system of language. *Syntactic* or *structural* information comes from knowing how words are organized in the flow of language. Readers draw on the knowledge of grammar they have internalized when learning to talk to predict what words are likely to appear next.

Using the Teacher's Notes (continued)

Graphophonic information refers to the relationship between letters, clusters of letters, and their corresponding sounds.

Linguists have identified single sounds as *phonemes.* *Phonemic awareness* is the ability to hear sounds in words and identify particular sounds.

At any one time, readers will be using a combination of these cues to sample, predict, confirm, and self-correct as they read or process text. The teaching notes provided for each book explicitly model ways to support children in the use of these sources of information.

The first example shows how use of the cue systems is supported in the teaching notes for the text *Communities.*

Semantic
Discuss what communities are. Draw on children's experiences to talk about housing, jobs, schools, and shopping in their community.

Syntactic
Have children look for the pattern the author uses to communicate the information.

Using the Teacher's Notes (continued)

Graphophonic
Have children check the print to confirm or self-correct their answers.

A Rural Community

This house is in a rural community. A rural community is in the country, and the houses are often far apart. This house has fields and farms around it.
2

In a rural community, some people live on farms. Others may live in the nearby towns. This is a rural town. People work in the banks, restaurants, offices, and stores here.

3

These additional examples show how children are supported to recognize and use the different cue systems.

Semantic
Coming to America Have children skim to find where the people were waiting. Ask: *How would you feel if you were waiting on Ellis Island after a long journey?*

Syntactic
The Pueblo People Have children identify the key words *long ago* and *today* that signal the pattern.

Going West Discuss why each item on the chart has only one picture but some have plural spellings.

Graphophonic
Keeping Bees Ask: *Did the word* warm *help you to read any other word on these pages?* Discuss how *swarm* and *warm* are alike.

Rereading and discussing
This section focuses on ways in which the students can be encouraged to revisit the book or to read beyond the book as well as to reflect on the act of reading. Some of the suggestions or questions will provide a focus for the teacher's observations and assessment. However, it should be remembered that monitoring of newly introduced skills and strategies immediately following a first reading is at a superficial and recall level rather than an indication of the students' real understanding of the book or independent application of skills and strategies.

Social studies connections
These connections support and extend the concepts introduced in the books. Many activities provide children with opportunities to create maps, charts, and webs.

19

Reading and writing social studies

Here you will find ideas for further investigations that relate to and extend the concepts in each book. The emphasis is on understanding and applying concepts. The activities involve independent as well as collaborative investigations and observations, and the application of the concepts to the students' own world.

Home/school connections

These activities link the concept of each book to the wider world of home and community. They provide opportunities for children to continue observations and inquiries with their families and friends. Several of these activities require children to interpret and communicate information by reading and constructing maps, time lines, and charts. Others require them to make detailed observations of everyday life in their neighborhoods.

Additional resources

The bibliography of fiction and non-fiction books at the back helps you locate related books for inclusion in your social studies lessons and library center. Children will be able to read some books on their own. Others are appropriate for reading to the class. And still others can be used for "dipping into" to find facts and other related information.

Assessment

A separate assessment book is provided with the *Discovery Links* program containing both student and teacher reproducibles.

Teacher assessment tools consist of the following:

- Observational Profiles to gather ongoing data about students' reading behaviors and strategies.
- Student Oral Reading Assessments to assess the student's use of cueing systems.
- Student Retelling Assessments which assess comprehension on several different levels.

Student reproducibles include:

- Cloze exercises
- Diagrams
- Graphic organizers

Supporting the English Language Learner

Newbridge Discovery Links: Guided Reading Through Social Studies supports classrooms in which children do not necessarily share the same first language. The strong photo/text support enables teachers to bridge the gap often created by language and experience differences. The following features of *Discovery Links* make it ideally suited to your English language learners.

• The strong photo/text match helps build background and familiarity with topics *visually.*

• The focus on non-fiction promotes acquisition of content-area vocabulary and concepts at appropriate developmental levels.

• English language learners acquire practice with informational texts at the earliest opportunity, which ensures familiarity with key text features in preparation for more demanding texts at upper grades.

• The range of topics and books presented in *Discovery Links* supports opportunities for children from other cultures to be the primary contributors to some discussions and topics, as in the case of books like *We Celebrate.*

• Strong and consistent word-picture correspondence and rich visual cues support children's acquisition of language and concepts, as do the consistent language patterns of the texts.

Supporting the English Language Learner

English language learners will be more likely to take risks with their new language if they feel safe and secure. In a supportive atmosphere children will begin to feel more comfortable and ready to join in. The small-group situation of guided reading provides an ideal environment for children to learn oral and written language.

You might consider using the following strategies in working with English language learners:

The book *Coming to America* is a wonderful way to introduce children to the topic of moving to a new country and a way to encourage children to share their own experiences. Point out that America and the United States are used synonymously. *Our Capital* introduces children to Washington, D. C. Invite children to tell about the capital cities of their home countries. If they are not familiar with the capital cities, help them to find information to share with the group.

Invite children to compare their own family customs and traditions after reading *We Celebrate*. Write several additional pages for the book using the ideas suggested by the children.

Before reading *Looking at Money*, briefly introduce the people named in the text as important people from American history. Note that children from other cultures may not be familiar with American currency. Provide several opportunities for children to examine real coins and bills. Also, have children bring in currencies from other countries to compare and contrast.

When reading *Signs* point out that the information in a sign is often communicated with words and pictures so that even if a person cannot yet read the words, its message can be understood. Invite children to talk about signs that are familiar in their home countries. Along with *Signs*, the book *Communities* helps to generate interest in environmental print.

Use the books *The Pilgrims* and *Going West* to talk about two significant periods in American history. Help children compare the time periods using the books.

Young English language learners will blossom in an environment that is inclusive and supportive. This type of environment encourages the children to become involved in classroom activities as they gradually acquire an "ear" for the language. The guided reading process provides considerable advantages for working with English language learners because information is presented in an accessible manner.

Fluent Level Guided Reading Books

A City Grows	The Olympics
Coming to America	Our Capital
Communities	The Pilgrims
Going West	The Pueblo People
Good Neighbors	Reading Maps
How Paper Is Made	Shipping Goods
Keeping Bees	Signs
Landforms	The Statue of Liberty
Looking at Money	Taking Care of Trees
Making Choices	Volunteers
Maybe I Could	We Celebrate
National Parks	We Vote

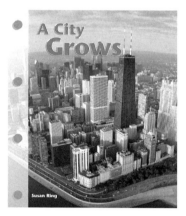

Susan Ring

Standards
Time, Continuity, and Change

Students will establish a sense of order and time by learning how the city of Chicago grew and changed from long ago to the present.

Supports
- easily decodable words
- moderate photo and illustration support

Challenges
- elaborated events
- time line requires detailed viewing

Text features
Structure: sequence

Visual text: time line

Language: sequence transitions: *four years later, by the 1850s, on the night of, in 1885, today*

Introducing the text
- Have children look at the title. Ask them which words describe what they see. Then ask which word describes what they will learn about a city.
- Focus discussion on the cover photograph. Ask children what might have changed in the city over the years.

The first reading

Title page: Have children compare this page with the cover photo. Ask: *What difference do you see? What has changed?* Invite children to look at both photos and tell what they can learn from each one.

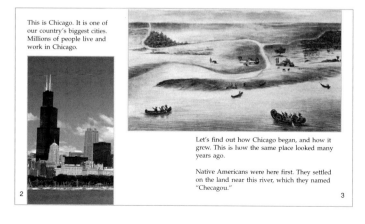

This is Chicago. It is one of our country's biggest cities. Millions of people live and work in Chicago.

Let's find out how Chicago began, and how it grew. This is how the same place looked many years ago.

Native Americans were here first. They settled on the land near this river, which they named "Checagou."

2

3

By the 1850s, Chicago had become a big city. It would soon become one of the largest lumber centers in the world.

Ten years later, the city had grown so much that, by the 1860s, it had fifteen railroad lines. Now it was easy for people to get to Chicago by water and land.

Many ranchers brought their cattle to Chicago stockyards to sell.

Pages 2-3: Read to find how Chicago got its name. Discuss why it was a good place to build a city.

Pages 4-5: Ask children to read to find out what Chicago started as and when. Have them find the words that tell them that Chicago was still not a city in 1833.

Pages 6-9: Have children survey the photos, then read these pages silently. Ask: *What did these pages tell you?* Afterward, suggest they think about what they read and how it adds to what they have already read.

Pages 10-11: Continue to support children to cross-check the information in the pictures and written text. Encourage them to draw inferences based on that information.

Pages 12-15: Discuss the materials used to build the modern Chicago. Ask: *How might these materials be better than wood?*

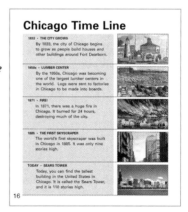

Chicago Time Line

Page 16: Model how to read the time line. Revisit individual pages to check the information on the time line.

Give children time to reread and review their books on their own. Observe how they apply skills and strategies to maintain meaning. Are they checking meaning from multiple sources of information?

Rereading and discussing

- Invite responses to the book. Focus a brief discussion on the parts of the book children particularly liked and on what they learned.
- Suggest children reread part of the book with a buddy. This time, have them focus on the ways the author has shown the sequence of events.
- Identify and list the time sequences the author used. Show how these were used to construct a time line and communicate the information in a graphic form.

Social studies connections

In this activity children will create a time line using specific years to present important facts they learned about Chicago.

- Have children work together to find and list each year mentioned in the book. List the years on the chalkboard: 1803, 1833, 1850s, 1860, 1870, 1871, 1885.
- Work together with children to reread what events occurred during each year listed.
- Have children choose 5 years they would like to include in a time line about Chicago.
- Draw a time line on chart paper as children draw their own time lines. Discuss how far each date should be from the next and why.
- Help children list each event in the appropriate place on their time line.
- Have children compare their time lines to the one on page 16.

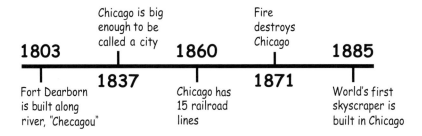

Reading and writing social studies

- Explore children's ideas about what they think their own town or street might have looked like 100 years ago. List ideas on the chalkboard.
- Have children use the list to copy and complete the following frame about their town or street:

  Years ago_____(name of town or street)_____had _____(description)_____.

  Today,_____(description of how it has changed)_____.

Home/school connections

- Encourage children to work with family members on a family time line. Family members can help children list special events in their family for 5 different dates or years. Encourage children to share their family time lines with the class.
- Invite children to take home the activity sheet from the home/school connections book to do in collaboration with their families.

Coming to America

Coming to America

Debra P. Hertkowitz

Standards
Global Connections

Students will learn about their historical roots by finding out when, why, and how people came to America.

Supports
- high percentage of high-frequency words

Challenges
- concepts
- interpreting information in photographs and map

Text features
Structure: description

Visual text: map

Organization: contents page, index

Language: proper nouns, past tense

Introducing the text

- Read the title with the children. Ask them to look at the clues in the cover photograph that help them know how the people have traveled to America, and how long ago the photograph was taken.
- Tell children that these people were making a long journey to make their homes in the United States.
- Read the back-cover blurb with them to establish what the book will help them learn.

The first reading

Contents page: Read the contents page to find the first topic.

Pages 2–3: Focus discussion on why Ellis Island was built. Have children silently read page 3 to find the words that tell where the people came from and how long it took to get there. Talk about what some of their hopes and dreams might have been.

This is Ellis Island. Long ago, many people who wanted to live in our country had to come here first.

2

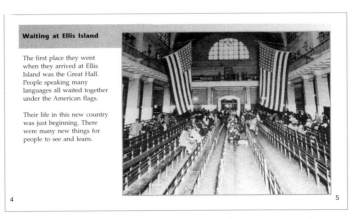

Pages 4-5:   Have children skim to find where the people were waiting. Ask: *How would you feel if you were waiting on Ellis Island after a long journey?*

Pages 6-11:   Scan the pictures. Discuss the new experiences the people were having in their new country.

Pages 12-13:   Talk about the information the map shows. Identify some of the places the people might travel to if they went in a specific direction. Ask: *Where might people leaving Ellis Island and traveling north go?*

Pages 14-15:   Ask children to read to find out what they can see at Ellis Island today. As they share their answers, encourage them to reread to check their information. Have children think back to the word the author used to describe these people. Ask: *Now that you have read the book, can you think of another word to use instead?*

Page 16:   Ask the children to use the index to locate specific information.

Invite children to use the index to choose several items to read again. As they silently read, ask individuals to read aloud for a minute or two. Are they using a variety of problem-solving strategies for unfamiliar or specialized vocabulary? Are they using phrasing?

Rereading and discussing

- Give the children time to talk and question among themselves. Proïvide support to discuss what they found interesting or important about the text.
- Choose a double-page spread and discuss some of the new experiences that can be inferred by looking at the photographs.
- Invite children to reread the book. This time ask them to think about why these people were so brave.

Social studies connections

In this activity children will explore different means of transportation used to travel to and from Ellis Island.

- Have a discussion about transportation. Make a list on chart paper of the various types children suggest:

> boats
>
> trains
>
> airplanes
>
> cars
>
> bicycles

- Have children revisit the photographs in the book and work together to mark the transportation vehicles they see that are on their list. Have them add any that are not on the list.
- On chart paper, work with the children to create a web showing the different modes of transportation used to get to and from Ellis Island.

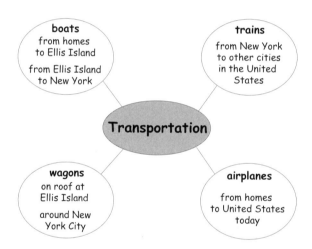

Reading and writing social studies

- Focus on the different methods of transportation in the web. Have children choose one means of transportation and find a page in the book that shows a photograph of it.
- Challenge children to pretend they are in the photo. Have them draw a picture of the means of transportation in the photograph and write a journal entry telling what they are doing or feeling.

Home/school connections

- Invite children to talk to family members about where their ancestors came from. Have children share what they found out with the group and show on a world map how far their ancestors traveled to get to the United States.
- Invite children to take home the activity sheet from the home/school connections book to do in collaboration with their families.

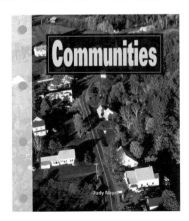

Standards
Individuals, Groups, and Institutions

Students will develop an understanding of how people meet their needs in three different types of communities: urban, suburban, and rural.

Supports
- repeating pattern of information
- some repetition of language

Challenges
- interpreting chart

Text features
Structure: compare/contrast

Organization: contents page, headings

Visual text: chart

Language: specialized language: *urban, suburban, rural*

Introducing the text
- Discuss what *communities* are. Draw on children's experiences to talk about housing, jobs, schools, and shopping in their community. Read the title and have children compare their experiences to the community pictured on the front cover.
- Read the blurb on the back cover together. Ask children what part of the book might list the three different kinds of communities.

The first reading
Contents page: Read the contents page together. Have children predict which word best describes their community. Find and check these pages and check the photos and text to confirm predictions. Establish the pattern used to communicate the information on these pages. Have children turn back to the contents page to find where to begin reading about a rural community.

Communities

Contents

Judy Nayer

Pages 2-5:	Have children skim these pages to establish that the pattern of information is the same as the pages they checked. Ask: *What do the photos tell you about where people live, work, shop, and go to school?* Have children check the print to confirm or self-correct their answer.	 In a suburban community, some children take the bus to school. Children may have a short bus ride to school because the school is not far from their homes. 8

Pages 6-13:   Continue to support children to skim and scan the information in the print and photos. Encourage them to turn back and reread previous text to help them read and compare the information about each community.

Pages 14-15:	Discuss how a chart works and how it provides an easy way to compare information as well as providing a summary. Encourage children to select a heading and describe what the pictures tell about each community in their own words.	
Page 16:	Read this page together. Invite children's responses to the question and discuss reasons for their responses.	In the United States, people might live in a rural, suburban, or urban community. They work, play, go to school, have fun, and share special times together there. Which kind of community do you live in? 16

Return to the contents page and invite children to choose which section they will read independently. Provide support where necessary to help them maintain or regain meaning. Observe strategies they use to problem-solve unfamiliar words and maintain momentum as they read. Are they using photos and text to confirm or self-correct?

Rereading and discussing

• Discuss points of interest for individuals as well as questions they might have as a result of reading the book.
• Use the framework of the chart to write about your community. Compare the advantages and disadvantages of living in your community with one of those described in the book.

Social studies connections

In this activity children will convert a picture chart to a word chart to compare different kinds of communities.

- Have children open the *Communities* book to the chart on pages 14 and 15.
- Work together with children to read the title of the chart and row and column headings.
- Have children draw a chart of their own on paper, as you draw one on chart paper that has the same title, row, and column headings as the chart on pages 14 and 15.
- Work together with children to complete their charts by using the pictures on pages 14 and 15 as well as returning to the appropriate pages in the book to help them write the words that belong in each row and column of the chart.
- Children can then use their charts to ask and answer questions about the different communities.

Three Kinds of Communities

	Where People Live	Where People Work	How Children Get to School	Where People Shop
Rural	farms	banks, stores	long bus ride	small stores
Suburban	houses	office buildings	short bus ride	shopping malls
Urban	apartment buildings	office buildings, factories	walk	supermarkets, small stores

Reading and writing social studies

- Take children on a walk around their community. Have them bring pencils and pads to jot down interesting buildings, stores, or other sights they see.
- Have children use their lists to choose one favorite place they observed, draw a picture of it, and write a sentence below the picture telling what it is and why they like it.

Home/school connections

- Encourage children to ask family members to complete the chart children made about communities with information about their life in their community: Where do they live? Where do they work? How do they get to work/school? Where do they shop? Encourage them to use names of specific places at which they work, live, and shop.
- Invite children to take home the activity sheet from the home/school connections book to do in collaboration with their families.

Going West

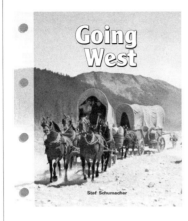

Stef Schumacher

Standards
Individuals, Groups, and Institutions

Students will develop an understanding of the experiences and hardships the pioneers endured as they traveled west, thus laying the foundation for the development of historical knowledge, skills, and values.

Supports
• moderate photo support
• sequential organization

Challenges
• extended description

Text features
Structure: problem/solution

Visual text: picture list

Organization: contents page, headings

Language: past-tense verbs: *traveled, packed, played, cooked, talked, reached, cleared*

Introducing the text

• Read and discuss the title and cover photograph. Ask what *Going West* means. Discuss how traveling like this would be different from how people travel today. Establish where the family is traveling from and to.

• Ask children what they expect to read about in this book.

• Read the information in the back-cover blurb. How is this information the same as or different from children's thinking?

The first reading

Contents page: Read the contents page together. Ask: *What would a family need to do to get ready for the journey?* List items they need to take. Have children turn back to the front cover. Focus on the size of the wagons. Ask: *Would all of the items on the list fit? What would they have to leave behind?*

Packing for the Trip
Here are some of the things a family might want to take.

flour, sugar, seeds

blankets

butter churn

chairs

lanterns

tools

pots and pans

candles

water barrels

stove

3

The ride could be bumpy. There were no real roads, just trails made by other wagons. Families traveled together. Their wagons formed a long line called a wagon train.

When the wagons were packed, the families were ready to begin their trip. They were going to travel across the country to start a new life.

4

5

Pages 2-3:   Have children read the picture list. Discuss why each item has only one picture but some have plural spellings.

Pages 4-5:   Have children skim the text to find out how people knew which way to go. Ask: *Why do you think the people traveled together in a wagon train?*

Pages 6-7:   Read the heading together. Remind children about the purpose of a heading. Have them predict what might happen during a day's travel.

Pages 8-13:   Continue to set purposes to guide the reading. Ensure that children understand that the pictures extend information in the text.

Pages 14-15:   Read the text together. Have children predict what the families will do next. Turn back to the list on page 3 to support the discussion.

The families cleared the land and built homes. They were ready to begin a new life on their new land.

16

Page 16:   Invite children to read this page independently. Discuss which of their predictions are reflected on this page.

Have children use the contents page to choose pages to read independently. Observe to see how effectively they use the table of contents and headings. Are they cross-checking information in the pictures and corresponding print?

Rereading and discussing

- Invite responses. Have children discuss what they learned.
- Encourage children to return to the pictures to support and extend their discussion.
- Browse through the book again, supporting inferencing by raising questions from the text and pictures. Ask: *What do the words* The ride could be bumpy *tell you?*

Social studies connections

In this activity children will use webs to create descriptions of the different topics presented in the book.

- Have children return to the contents page. Discuss how many topics the book presents and how the contents page helps them know this.
- Work together with children to create a word web that gives descriptive words about the first topic: *Getting Ready to Go*.
- Have volunteers use the word web to give oral descriptions of what they know about the first topic.
- Continue working with children to create a word web for each of the remaining topics and use each to help children give oral presentations about what they have learned.

Reading and writing social studies

- Display the word webs children made for the different topics covered in the book.
- Invite children to choose one topic and use the contents page to return to that section of the book.
- Have children pretend they are part of the wagon train they have read about in the section they chose.
- Have them write a journal entry describing an experience they might have had as part of the group going west. Remind them to use the word webs to help. Tell children to begin their entry with *Dear Diary,*

    Today_____
- Invite volunteers to share their entries with the group.

Home/school connections

- Encourage children to ask family members to describe trips they have taken by telling how they packed and prepared for the trip, where they went, and what hardships they may have had.
- Invite children to take home the activity sheet from the home/school connections book to do in collaboration with their families.

Standards
Global Connections

Students will explore and examine global connections by comparing the geographical location and points of interest of Mexico and Canada.

Supports
- moderate photo support
- many high-frequency words

Challenges
- interpreting and applying information in a map
- specific vocabulary: country, city, and building names

Text features
Structure: compare/contrast

Organization: contents page, headings

Visual text: map, e-mail letters, flags, fact boxes

Language: first person

Introducing the text
- After reading the title, speculate how it relates to the cover photographs. Introduce the idea of people in two countries being good neighbors. Have children tell what clues in the photographs support this idea.
- When children identify the Canadian flag, have them think about which countries are Canada's neighbors.
- Read the back-cover blurb and discuss how this adds to the cover information. Predict what Pat and Maria might tell each other about their countries.

The first reading

Contents page: Talk about the photograph and support inferential thinking. Ask: *What information does the picture add? How does it help you think about distance, time, and the mountains?* Read the contents page to find what the first topic is.

Good Neighbors

Contents

Max Winter

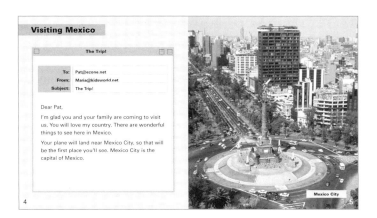

Pages 2-3: Guide discussion about the information in the map and text. Ask: *How does this confirm or change your thinking about the contents-page photo?*

Pages 4-9: Set a purpose for skimming and scanning the photos and text. Ask: *What important information is Maria telling about her country?* Encourage rereading to check responses. Invite children to visualize Mexico from the photos and descriptions. Ask: *How is it different from and the same as where you live?*

Pages 10-11: Have children read this page silently. Compare the information with where Maria lives.

Pages 12-15: Ask: *Why is Pat telling Maria about Quebec as well as Alberta? How is the old place in his country different from the old places Maria has described?*

Page 16: Read and compare the facts about each country.

Our Neighbors: Canada and Mexico

CANADA

Capital:	Ottawa
Official Languages:	English and French
Population:	29,123,194 (as of 1998)
Highest Point:	Mount Logan (19,524 feet)
Geography:	3,849,674 square miles. Canada is the largest country in North America.

MEXICO

Capital:	Mexico City
Official Language:	Spanish
Population:	97,563,374 (as of 1998). Mexico has the second largest population in North America.
Highest Point:	Orizaba Mountain (18,701 feet)
Geography:	758,136 square miles

16

Invite children to choose part of the book to read independently. Observe their reading strategies. Are they using effective strategies to decode unfamiliar words? Are they utilizing the information in the map and photographs? Are they noticing and using punctuation?

Rereading and discussing

• Invite discussion about the children's responses to the book. As they revisit the book, point out the way Pat and Maria compare and contrast their two countries.

• Write *Canada* and *Mexico* as headings for two columns on chart paper. Rewrite the information on page 16 so that it is aligned on the chart. Then add information from the book. Suggest children continue to add information over several days.

• Focus discussion on strategies for reading and pronouncing *Rue* and *Quebec*.

37

Social studies connections

Children will use critical thinking skills to expand on what they learned in the book.

Materials: markers, construction paper, scissors, glue, travel brochures, resources for additional information such as atlases and encyclopedias (online and/or hard copy)

- Show children examples of different travel brochures.
- Discuss the kind of information they contain. Establish that people use travel brochures to help them decide which places to visit.
- Divide the group into two smaller groups and assign one country (Canada, Mexico) to each.
- Explain that each group will create a travel brochure about their country.
- To help children create their brochures, brainstorm a list of information they might want to include: description of points of interest, location, language, climate.

- Give groups time to plan and create their brochures over several days. Encourage them to include pictures and reasons why their country would be fun to visit.
- Provide guidance as group members work on their brochures.
- When completed, have groups share their brochures with each other as well as with other classes.

Reading and writing social studies

- Have children revisit the e-mail letters shown on pages 4–14.
- Invite them to use them as models to write an e-mail to a friend, inviting him or her to visit the United States.
- Have children share their e-mail letters with the group.

Home/school connections

- Encourage children to plan an imaginary trip to Mexico or Canada with a family member. Invite them to tell each other when they would go, how long they would stay, where they would visit, and why.
- Invite children to take home the activity sheet from the home/school connections book to do in collaboration with their families.

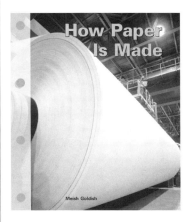

Standards
Science, Technology, and Society

Students will learn the process of making paper and how newspapers are made and distributed.

Supports
• large percentage of high-frequency words

Challenges
• extended descriptions
• transitions that signal sequences

Text features
Structure: sequence

Organization: table of contents, headings, index

Language: sequence transitions: *first, then, the next step, when, now, the last step*

Introducing the text
• Read the title and discuss how the author might share this information.
• Use the back-cover blurb as a framework for drawing on prior knowledge and experience to discuss what the children already know about the topic.

The first reading

Contents page: Read the table of contents together. Compare it with the discussion you just had. Ask: *Does the table of contents include topics you expected? Where else in the book could you check the content?* Guide children to suggest the index. Then ask: *What do you need to know to use an index effectively?* Establish that because this book relates a sequence of steps in a process, it is necessary to read from front to back. Use the contents page to find where to begin reading about the first topic.

How Paper Is Made

Contents

Meish Goldish

Pages 2-3:	Have children read these pages silently.

First, trees are cut down and chopped into logs. The logs are then shipped to a factory called a paper mill. There the wood will be made into paper.

5

Pages 4-5:	Set a purpose for these pages by asking children to keep a list of the facts the author has included. Encourage them to read and reread to check these facts before sharing them.
Pages 6–9:	Have children skim these pages to locate any words they are unsure of. Encourage them to share their problem-solving strategies. Discuss the meaning of the specialized words.
Pages 10-11:	Have children read silently before reviewing the steps followed in the process of paper making.
Pages 12-13:	Continue to support independent reading.
Pages 14-15:	Discuss paper products children use.
Page 16:	Use the index to find specific information.

Give children time to skim through the chapter headings or index to revisit and review part of the book on their own. Observe how they use these organizational features to locate information and the problem-solving strategies they apply to unfamiliar words and concepts.

Rereading and discussing

- Ask children to choose a partner to work with and assign a different purpose for each pair to revisit in the book. For example:
  Read to find out how and why the bark is removed.
  Read to find out how pulp is made.
  Read to find out how the water is separated from the soggy wood pulp.
- Have children share their information and describe how they located it.

Social studies connections

In this activity children will play a game in which they must order the steps in the process of making paper.

- Have children brainstorm a list of steps involved in the process of making paper.
- Write each step suggested on its own index card.
- Work together to read and order the index cards by placing them in order along the edge of the chalkboard.
- Then collect the cards and shuffle them.
- Have each child take a turn ordering the cards along the chalkboard edge.
- You may wish to use a stopwatch and time each child as he or she orders the steps. You can then compare times to see who ordered the cards the fastest.

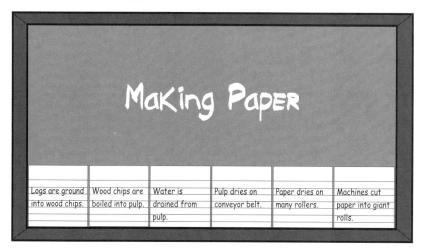

Making Paper

Logs are ground into wood chips.	Wood chips are boiled into pulp.	Water is drained from pulp.	Pulp dries on conveyor belt.	Paper dries on many rollers.	Machines cut paper into giant rolls.

Reading and writing social studies

- Have children look around the classroom to identify paper products they use in school. List the products on chart paper.
- Have children use the list to draw a picture of themselves using one of the products and then write a sentence telling how they are using the paper product in their picture.

Home/school connections

- Encourage children to work with family members to list as many paper products as they can that they use in their home. Have children bring in their lists to share.
- Invite children to take home the activity sheet from the home/school connections book to do in collaboration with their families.

Standards
Production, Distribution, and Consumption

Students will learn how beekeepers raise bees that produce honey and beeswax and how these products are used by consumers.

Supports
- strong photo/text match
- many high-frequency words

Challenges
- variety of sentence structures
- specialized language

Text features
Structure: sequence

Organization: table of contents, headings, index

Visual text: flowchart, chart

Language: *nectar, swarm, beeswax, hive, honeycomb*

Introducing the text
- Discuss the cover photograph and title. Ask children to tell what information they communicate.
- Read the back-cover blurb together and encourage children to predict how the bees and beekeeper help each other.

The first reading

Contents page: Scan the table of contents. Encourage children to briefly share what they know about each entry.

Pages 2-3: Read the heading, then have children silently read. Ask: *Did the word* warm *help you to read any other word on these pages?* Discuss how *swarm* and *warm* are alike. Have children predict where the beekeeper will put the box. Remind them that the cover photo can help their thinking.

A New Hive

This swarm of buzzing bees and their queen are searching for the best place to build a new hive.

The swarm flies into the beekeeper's box. The warm, dry box is a good place for a hive. Now the bees can get to work making honey.

2

3

Pages 4-5:	Invite children to read these pages to check their prediction.
Pages 6-7:	Ask: *What do bees get from flowers? What do they build to store their honey?* Discuss using parts of known words, such as "tar" in *nectar*, to help read unknown words.

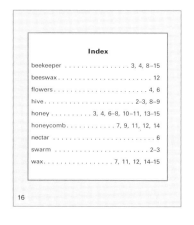

Bees and Flowers

Bees collect nectar from flowers and use it to make honey. Honey is food for the bees.

6

Pages 8-9:	Skim the text and photos on page 8. Discuss what the word *quiet* means here. Ask: *Why does the beekeeper want the bees quiet? Which words tell us that the bees will not be harmed?* Read page 9 to find another reason the beekeeper is careful.
Pages 10-13:	Have children silently read these pages and think how the beekeeper and bees help each other.
Pages 14-15:	Point out how the flowchart helps organize and communicate the information.
Page 16:	Use the index to locate some specific information.

Index

16

Give the group time to choose and read several pages to themselves. Observe what interests individual children as they do this, as well as the strategies they use to maintain meaning as they read.

Rereading and discussing

- Follow the lead of the children as you support discussion of their questions and comments about the book.
- Revisit several pages to model and invite inferencing from the text and photos. List ways the bees and beekeeper helped each other.
- Encourage children to work with a partner, each taking turns to read a chapter.

Social studies connections

In this activity children will create cards and use them to play a game to practice ordering the steps that show what happens to honey "from the beehive to the store."

- Display 5 blank index cards.
- Revisit the book with children.
- Work together to list on the cards each step a beekeeper follows to raise bees and collect the honey and wax, as shown below.
- Shuffle the cards and give one card to each member of the group.
- Have children work together to arrange themselves in the correct order based on the card they are holding.
- You may wish to repeat this activity several times and use a stopwatch to see how quickly children can order themselves and the steps each time.

Beekeeper puts boxes near flowers.	Swarm of bees flies into beekeeper's box.	Bees make honey and honeycomb made of wax.

Beekeeper collects honey and wax.	Beekeeper sells honey and wax.

Reading and writing social studies

- Bring in a jar of honey for children to observe, touch, and/or taste.
- Have them brainstorm a list of as many words as they can that describe the honey. List the words in a web:

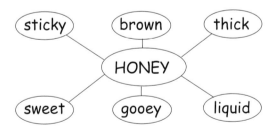

- Children can then each write a sentence about honey using the word web they created. Have them share their sentences orally with each other.

Home/school connections

- Encourage children to ask family members if they have ever used a product made with honey or beeswax. Have them take a survey to see how many family members like or do not like honey. Children can share and combine the results of their surveys with the group.
- Invite children to take home the activity sheet from the home/school connections book to do in collaboration with their families.

44

Landforms

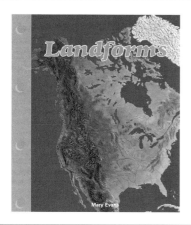

Mary Evans

Standards
People, Places, and Environments

Students will build a basis for creating geographic perspectives on the world by identifying characteristics of the different landforms.

Supports
• strong photo support
• many high-frequency words

Challenges
• concepts

Text features
Structure: compare/contrast

Organization: bolded words, labels

Visual text: picture glossary

Language: *bay, canyon, cliff, desert, hills, island, mesa, mountains, peninsula, plain, valley, volcano*

Introducing the text

• Read the title and the back-cover blurb. Identify and discuss the landforms shown in the photo on the cover. List them on chart paper. Establish that landform maps use color symbols to show different kinds of land and water.

• Talk about landforms in your state and community and add them to your list. Encourage children to think how they would define and describe the different landforms.

The first reading

Title page: Skim the title page. Add landforms seen here to the list.

Sawtooth Mountains and Salmon River, Idaho

We can see many different landforms on the Earth. A landform is a natural area that is part of the Earth's surface.

2   3

Pages 2-3:   Have children read silently before discussing what the word *natural* means here. Identify the natural landforms in the photograph.

Grand Canyon, Arizona

A **canyon** is a landform made by a river. Over time, the river cuts steep walls into the rock. This is the Grand Canyon. People from all over the world visit the Grand Canyon. It is in Arizona.

5

Pages 4-5:   Point out that landforms are in bold print. Remind children of definitions they talked about for other landforms. Invite them to find the author's definition for *bay* and *canyon*. Guide children to read these pages independently. Encourage children to reread each page to identify its information. Introduce the picture glossary on page 16. Compare the glossary information with the definitions on each page.

Pages 6-7:   Challenge children to find and share the definitions of each landform. Read the labels on each photograph. Ensure children understand their role.

Pages 8-11:   Continue to support children to read and understand these pages. Encourage them to read the labels to see how they confirm and often extend the information in the running text.

Pages 12-15:   Continue supporting group members to use effective strategies to comprehend the text. Use the glossary to define bolded words.

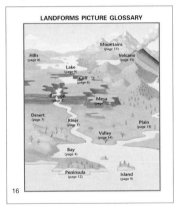

LANDFORMS PICTURE GLOSSARY

Mountains (page 11)
Hills (page 8)
Volcano (page 15)
Lake (page 6)
Cliff (page 10)
Canyon (page 5)
Mesa (page 10)
Desert (page 7)
River (page 5)
Plain (page 13)
Valley (page 14)
Bay (page 4)
Peninsula (page 12)
Island (page 9)

16

Page 16:   Discuss the different landforms shown on the map. Use the picture glossary to aid discussion.

Provide time for children to review the book before inviting them each to choose two pages to read independently. Observe and support strategies for maintaining meaning and forward movement. Do they use known words and parts of words to solve unfamiliar words?

Rereading and discussing

- Encourage discussion and inferential thinking. Ask children what they liked and what they learned from the text and photographs.
- Ask children each to select a page to read to a buddy.
- Invite children to consider other ways of communicating the information and explore this with several pages. Discuss whether or not a chart or web would convey the information effectively and why.

Social studies connections

In this activity children will label a map and create a map key to identify locations of a variety of landforms throughout the United States.

Materials: labeled outline map of the 48 contiguous United States

- Display a large outline map of the United States.
- Revisit page 16 in the book. Have children choose and list 5 landforms they read about in the book.
- Work together to locate the first landform in the book to find out where it is located in the United States.
- Have children share ideas about how that landform can be represented in a key on your map.
- List the landform symbol in a key and in the appropriate state on your map.
- Repeat with the other landforms on the children's list.

Reading and writing social studies

- Have each child make up a riddle describing a landform.
- Have them write their riddle on one side of an index card, and the answer on the other side. Children can then read and try to solve each other's riddles.
- Use the following as a model for children to follow:

    Front: I can be hot or cold. I am always dry. It almost never rains on me. What am I?

    Back: A desert

Home/school connections

- Provide each child with a small amount of clay and a list of landforms. Encourage children to work together with a family member to build a model of one landform in the list. Have children bring in their models to share with the class.
- Invite children to take home the activity sheet from the home/school connections book to do in collaboration with their families.

47

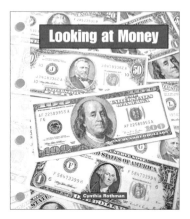

Looking at Money

Cynthia Rothman

Standards
Power, Authority, and Governance

A foundation will be laid for students' development of historical knowledge by presenting information about famous American historical figures that are represented on American currency.

Supports
• repetitive text pattern

Challenges
• historical figures

Text features
Structure: description

Organization: table of contents, headings

Visual text: money, chart

Language: proper nouns

Introducing the text

• Read the title and the back-cover blurb. Talk about the cover. Ask children to identify people they see and why they think their pictures are on money. Establish that this is one way we honor and remember our nation's leaders.

• Look at some coins and bills and identify the people pictured on each. Remind children about the history associated with a few of them.

The first reading

Contents page: Skim the table of contents. Ask: *What page will tell us about a penny? a half-dollar? a ten-dollar bill?*

Pages 2-3: Remind children that an introduction sets the scene for the content to come. Have them find the words that tell what we will read about.

Have you ever wondered about the faces you see on coins and bills? They are pictures of people who were important to our country. Let's read about these people.

3

Pages 4-5:	Invite children to survey these pages to find the pattern the author has used to communicate the information. Establish that each page tells who, which, and why. Have children share the information about each person.

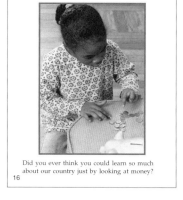

Quarter

This is George Washington. His picture is on a quarter.

George Washington was the first president of the United States. He was called "The Father of Our Country" because he helped build our new country.

7

Pages 6-7: Ask: *Has the author kept the same pattern? Whom is she telling us about here? What is she telling about them?*

Pages 8-9: Ask: *Why is John F. Kennedy's picture on this coin? Why do we honor Susan B. Anthony?*

Pages 10-13: Continue to support children to decode names and to read why these people are important to the history of our country.

Page 14-15: Read the heading and ask what it means. Have children use the chart to find out which year their state's new quarter will be issued. Ask: *What picture might it have to symbolize our state?*

Did you ever think you could learn so much about our country just by looking at money?
16

Page 16: Read this page together.

Invite children to reread several pages of their choice. Observe their reading strategies. Are they using the consistent pattern of the text to maintain fluency? Are they using known words as anchors to help solve unfamiliar words? Are they using a range of strategies flexibly and appropriately?

Rereading and discussing

- Discuss children's questions and observations. Ask if there were any people they had never heard of. Discuss how they could find out more about them. Have children tell if there are other people they would like to see honored on a coin or bill and explain why.
- Invite children to share their strategies for working out unfamiliar words.
- Encourage children to reread several pages independently or with a buddy.

Social studies connections

In this activity children will create and share webs to show the information they learned in the book.

- Have children revisit the contents page.
- Model how to create a word web for the information presented about a penny. Remind children that the pattern the author has used to communicate the information is by telling who, which, and why on each page.

- Divide the remaining topics equally among pairs of group members so that each pair is assigned 2 or 3 coins or bills as listed in the table of contents.
- Have partners work together to make a word web for each coin or bill they are assigned.
- Have partners present their webs to the group and orally share the information contained in each.

Reading and writing social studies

- Have children reread page 15 to find out what kind of design each of the new state quarters will have.
- Challenge children to design their own coin for their state.
- Have them draw a picture of the side featuring their state and write one or more words on their design to describe the coin.
- Have children share their designs with the group.

Home/school connections

- Invite children to ask family members whom they would put on coins and bills if they could design them. Encourage them to find out why.
- Invite children to take home the activity sheet from the home/school connections book to do in collaboration with their families.

Making Choices

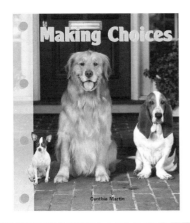

Standards
Production, Distribution, and Consumption

Students will explore the process of learning how to make choices and applying the process to personal situations.

Supports
- many high-frequency words
- familiar experiences

Challenges
- concepts
- integrating information from charts, lists, and running text

Text features
Structure: problem/solution

Visual text: lists, charts

Language: *choose, choice, chooses, choices*

Introducing the text
- Have children work out the title. Draw on their prior knowledge to discuss everyday choices they make and how they make them. Read the back-cover blurb and talk about what they give up when they make choices.
- Look at the cover picture. Have children tell how they would choose among these three dogs. Have them share what they would have to think about, what they would gain, and what they would give up.

The first reading

Title page: Invite children to look at the photo and speculate about what choices they would have to make.

Pages 2-3:   After briefly talking about the pictures, have children silently read these pages and then tell about what they read in their own words.

Pages 4-5:   Ask: *What has Maria done here to help her make a choice about what game to play?* Have children read why she made those choices. Then reread to confirm their answer to the question.

| *Pages 6-7:* | Skim these pages to find what Donna has to choose between. Discuss how she might decide. |

Donna has a school project she needs to finish in three days.

Her sister wants Donna's help with a puzzle.

How will she decide which one to choose?

7

| *Pages 8-11:* | Continue to support children to read and respond to these pages. |

| *Pages 12-15:* | Skim and scan to find the choices. Share the information and compare the advantages and disadvantages from the lists. Based on the comparisons, predict what each girl will choose and why. |

Sara and Jenny both picked just the right pet for their families. This is the pet they chose.

How did they decide which pet to choose?

16

| *Page 16:* | Have children read this page independently to check their predictions. |

Give children time to reread and review several pages. Observe their strategies for accessing the information. Are they reading the information in lists and charts? Are they integrating this with the information in the running text? Are they thinking about the reasons for the choices?

Rereading and discussing

- Discuss the children's responses to the book. Have them share what they liked, what they learned, and how the charts and lists helped them to think about the choices.
- Revisit and reread pages 12 and 13. Explore other ways of recording the information and making a decision.
- Investigate the words *choose, choice, chooses, choices.* Identify other words that can be built from these.
- Have children reread a few pages independently or with a friend.

Social studies connections

In this activity children will apply what they learned about making choices to their own lives.

- Invite the group to brainstorm a list of choices they have had to make recently. Display the list on a chart.

Choices we had to make
What to bring for lunch
Which book to read
When to do homework
Whom to ask for help with homework
What to wear to school

- Reread the list and have the group vote on one choice to explore.
- Revisit page 13 in the book and work together to create a chart about their choice using headings similar to those shown on the chart.

When to do homework	Good things	Bad things
Right after school	It will be finished early	No time to play right after school
Right after supper	I will have more energy to concentrate	Can't watch my favorite television program
Just before bedtime	I will have had time to play and talk to friends on phone	Too tired to work

- Brainstorm ideas to include in the chart.
- Use the chart to discuss which is the best choice and why.
- Encourage children to identify what they will give up by making this choice.

Reading and writing social studies

Materials: old magazines or brochures, scissors, glue

- Have children think about one career choice they are considering to follow when they grow up.
- Invite them to look through magazines to find pictures of people in this career, or to draw a picture to show this career. Have children cut out the pictures and paste them on construction paper.
- Children can then write one or two sentences to tell why they think this career might be a good choice for them.

Home/school connections

- Encourage children to talk to family members about why their family chose to live in this town or city.
- Invite children to take home the activity sheet from the home/school connections book to do in collaboration with their families.

Maybe I Could

Mary Martin

Standards
Individual Development and Identity

Students will explore their own development and identity by learning about the patterns of behavior evident in people in different careers.

Supports
- many short sentences
- repetitive text structure

Challenges
- specialized vocabulary: *botanist, zoologist*

Text features
Structure: compare/contrast

Language: compound words, first-person account

Introducing the text
- Have children read the title and think about the information in the cover photo. Ask them how the title and photograph go together. Have children tell who in the picture is thinking "Maybe I could" and what he is thinking he could do.
- Read the back-cover blurb together. Establish that the things children like to do now could be related to the jobs they do when they grow up.

The first reading

Title page: Invite children to speculate about what the doctor might have liked to do as a child.

Pages 2–3:   Have children read to find why the boy likes to go to the seashore. Ask: *What do you notice about the words* seashells *and* starfish*?* Have children read page 3 silently before discussing why the boy might like to be a deep-sea diver.

I like to go to the seashore. Sometimes I find seashells. Sometimes I find starfish. One time I found a crab.

2

54

Pages 4-7:	Continue to support skimming and scanning to locate information in the words and pictures.

Maybe I could become a zoologist and study animals. I would go to the places where animals live and watch them. I would take pictures of baby animals with their parents. I might write a book or make a movie about them.

Pages 8-9:	Discuss what *act like their parents* means, and have children share examples they know about. Have children scan the text to find the words that describe what a zoologist does.

9

Pages 10-15:	Focusing on the pattern the author has used to communicate the information, invite children to silently read these pages. Encourage them to notice and use punctuation to support fluent, phrased reading.

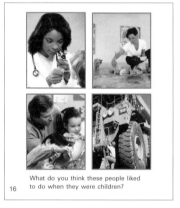

Page 16:	Invite discussion about what these people may have liked to play as children.

16 What do you think these people liked to do when they were children?

Give the group time to individually read and review their books. Observe their use of skills and strategies. Are they self-correcting close to the point of error? Do they notice and effectively use punctuation? Are they rereading to check and confirm?

Rereading and discussing

- Invite responses to the book. Focus discussion on the pages that relate to children's questions and comments.
- Have children choose several pages to reread either independently or with a buddy. Ask them to think about how the pattern of information supports their reading.
- Discuss how words and parts of words they know and understand help them to solve unknown words.

Social studies connections

In this activity children will compare activities they enjoy as children with activities involved in different careers.

- Have children revisit the book as you work together to complete a chart.
- Compare the activities the children do to the activities adults do in the different jobs presented in the book.
- Encourage children to include activities they like now and compare them to activities in careers they might want to follow as adults.

Job	Activities as a Child	Activities as an Adult
Deep-sea Diver	dig, find seashells and fish	search the ocean for seashells and fish
Pilot	make model airplanes, imagine flying in a plane	fly and land airplanes
Chef	make breakfast, make food for family	learn to make food taste good, make food in a restaurant

Reading and writing social studies

- Have children use the chart to discuss different activities they enjoy doing now.
- Work together to brainstorm a list of different jobs they might want to pursue as adults based on the activities they enjoy now.
- Children can then draw a picture to show themselves doing one job and write a sentence using the sentence frame below:

  Now I like to _____. When I grow up, maybe I could be a

  _____.

Home/school connections

- Encourage children to interview a family member about what he or she liked to do as a child. Have them compare those activities to what the family member does now as a career or a hobby.
- Invite children to take home the activity sheet from the home/school connections book to do in collaboration with their families.

National Parks

Mary Evans

Standards

People, Places, and Environments

Students will develop an understanding of the importance and location of various national parks, including the natural resources and geographic features of each.

Supports
- repetitive text structure

Challenges
- elaborated events

Text features

Structure: descriptive

Organization: contents page, headings, glossary, bolded words

Visual text: map, map key, compass rose

Language: specialized language: *national, rangers, glaciers, sandstone, arches, geyser, cougar, swamp*

Introducing the text

- Read the title and back-cover blurb together. Through discussion, establish what national parks are and why they are important.
- Survey the pages to establish the role of park rangers and to identify natural resources in each park and the ways people can enjoy them.

The first reading

Contents page: Have children skim the table of contents. Ask: On *which page would you begin reading about Glacier National Park? Everglades National Park?* Suggest reading *Visiting National Parks* first.

Visiting National Parks

Our **national** parks belong to all of us. The land, water, and wildlife in our national parks are protected for all of us to enjoy.

Pages 2-3:	Have children read page 2. Ask: *What do you think the word* protected *means on this page?* Have children skim page 3 to identify the jobs park rangers do. Discuss why *national* and *rangers* are in bold print. Ask: *Where might the author tell more about these words?* Turn to the glossary and read the definitions together. Note the alphabetic organization.

People can camp out in some national parks. They can sleep in a tent or a camper. Visitors to national parks may find that many other people want to visit there, too.

4

Pages 4-5:	Have children read silently to find a problem people who camp out might have. Discuss the other information the sign provides. Remind children that the rest of the contents can be read in any order. Then return to the contents page to choose which part to read next.
Pages 6-13:	Read one more entry as a group. Identify the pattern the author uses to structure the information. Ask: *Which part of the text tells what is special about the park? Which part tells what you can see and do there?* Practice using the glossary. Invite children to return to the contents page and choose another entry to read or review silently. Support them to do this.

Glossary

arches: curved structures

cougar: a large wild animal that is part of the cat family

geyser: a hole in the ground through which hot water shoots up

glaciers: huge sheets of ice that are formed at the tops of mountains

national: something that is national belongs to a nation or country

rangers: people in charge of a park or forest

sandstone: a kind of rock made up of quartz sand

swamp: a large, wet place where trees and bushes grow

16

Pages 14-15:	Use the map to find the national park nearest to where you live. Encourage children to use the compass rose to describe its location in relation to yours.
Page 16:	Review the purpose of the glossary.

Invite children to choose another entry to read independently. Observe how effectively they use the table of contents and glossary. What strategies do they use to figure out unfamiliar words? Do they reread to check for meaning?

Rereading and discussing

- Discuss individual responses to the book. Invite children to share their favorite part of the book with a buddy.
- Browse through the book again together with the children. Challenge them to define the bolded words before checking and confirming the definitions in the glossary.

Social studies connections

In this activity children will use a map to plan a trip in which they will visit each park presented in the book.

- Have children open *National Parks* to the contents page. List the names of the parks presented on chart paper.
- Next, turn to pages 14–15. Discuss the information they can learn from the map key and compass rose. Ask: *What does a green square mean on the map? How can you use the compass rose to help tell direction?*
- Discuss the following questions as children use the map and compass rose to plan a trip in which they visit Glacier, Arches, Yellowstone, and Everglades National Parks.

  Which park is the farthest north? the farthest south?

  Where should we begin our trip? Why?

  Where will we end our trip? Why?
- Work together with children to complete a flowchart showing the order and direction they will travel as they visit each park.

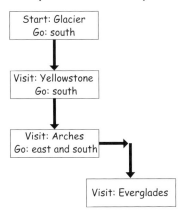

Reading and writing social studies

- Invite each child to choose one national park presented in the book. Have them write the name of the park on an index card. On the back of the card, help children list 2 to 4 facts about the park. Children can take turns reading their facts to the group as the others guess which park is being described.

Home/school connections

- Encourage children to ask family members if they have ever been to a national park or if they would like to visit one. Tell children to share with their family the name of one national park they read about that they would like to visit and why.
- Invite children to take home the activity sheet from the home/school connections book to do in collaboration with their families.

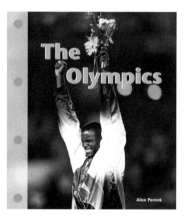

Alice Pernick

Standards
Time, Continuity, and Change

Students will learn about the history of the Olympics and how they have both changed and remained the same over time.

Supports
- moderate to strong photo support
- many high-frequency words

Challenges
- time span
- variety of sentence structures

Text features
Structure: compare/contrast

Organization: table of contents, headings, index

Visual text: labels

Language: past and present tense

Introducing the text
- Read the title and have children share what they know about Olympic Games. Establish that people from around the world compete in many sporting events.
- Read the back-cover blurb. Define the word *traditions*.

The first reading
Contents page: Check the table of contents. Ask: *Which topic might tell about a tradition related to the games?* Browse through the book to identify headings, to briefly discuss photos, and to obtain an overview of the content.

Introduction

The Olympic Games are held around the world. In 1996, the games were held in the United States, but the very first Olympic Games were held almost 3,000 years ago in a country called Greece.

A torch was lit at the beginning of those first Olympic Games. The torch stayed lit until the games were over.

Atlanta, 1996

2

3

Pages 2-3:   Ask: *What does the label tell you about the photo?* Discuss the role of a label. Ask: *Which words in the text tell you more about the photo?* Have children identify the important information they need to remember about the torch.

How the Games Began

In the very first Olympics, there was just one race. Runners ran to see who was the fastest. In later Greek Olympics, there were other contests. Riders raced in chariot races like these.

4

Pages 4-5:   Ask: *Which words has the author used to tell you when riders raced in chariot races like these?* Have children share their strategies for checking their thinking.

Pages 6-9:   Encourage children to look for clues in the photos before checking the text to find ways the Olympic Games changed.

Pages 10-13:   Challenge the group to locate the Olympic traditions described on these pages.

Pages 14-15:   Read the heading together before children read these pages independently. Ask: *What early tradition did the medals replace?*

Page 16:   Support children to use the index.

Invite children to return to the contents page to choose which entry they will review and read independently. Observe their reading strategies. Are they rereading to check understanding? Are they reading silently most of the time? Are they solving unfamiliar words without losing overall meaning?

Rereading and discussing

• Support discussion of individual responses to the book. Encourage children to tell what they found most interesting and why, what they learned, and what questions they have.
• Browse through the book to identify Olympic traditions and the different ways the author has communicated that information over a time sequence.

Social studies connections

In this activity children will create a compare/contrast chart about the Olympics today and in the past and discuss their similarities and differences.

- Head two columns on chart paper: *First Olympics; Olympics Today.*
- Work together with children to revisit each section of the book and list appropriate information under each heading.
- Encourage children to refer to the completed chart to discuss and answer questions about how the first Olympics have changed and how they remained the same compared to the Olympics of today.
- Ask questions such as:
  How are the games of the past the same as today?
  How are they different?
  Where did the athletes in the first Olympics come from?
  Where do they come from today?

First Olympics	Olympics Today
3,000 years ago	Every four years
Torch stayed lit until games were over	Torch stays lit until games are over
One race involving runners	Many different games such as shot put, skating
Winners got a crown	Winners get medals
Athletes from Greece	Athletes from many countries
No women athletes	1900: first women athletes

Reading and writing social studies

- Talk to children about games they have seen in the present-day Olympics or read about in this book.
- Have children draw a picture of their favorite game and write a descriptive sentence below it.
- Display pictures and sentences around the room.

Home/school connections

- Encourage children to talk with family members about their favorite Olympic events. Have them ask a family member: "If you could be an Olympic champion, which kind would you be?" Children can share family member responses with the group.
- Invite children to take home the activity sheet from the home/school connections book to do in collaboration with their families.

Our Capital

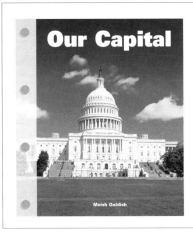

Our Capital

Meish Goldish

Standards
Power, Authority, and Governance

Students will develop an understanding of the significance and location of the various buildings and memorials in our nation's capital.

Supports
- high-frequency vocabulary to carry unfamiliar words
- repetition of some unfamiliar words

Challenges
- explanation of significance of each memorial

Text features
Structure: description

Visual text: map, map key

Organization: contents page, headings, index

Language: proper nouns, first-person account

Introducing the text
- Read and discuss the title and cover photograph. Establish what the children know about Washington, D.C. Ask what kind of information about the capital they expect to find in the book.
- Talk about the role of a blurb before having them read the information on the back cover. Then discuss how the blurb has supported or extended their thinking about the book.

The first reading

Contents page: Have children skim the table of contents. Ask: *Which chapter will tell you about the Capitol Building on the front cover?*

Pages 2-3: Invite children to match the chapter and page headings. Establish that the book is presented as a tour of the capital. Discuss the pattern the author has used to communicate the information about the Capitol Building.

The Capitol Building
Here is the Capitol Building. This is where our country's laws are made. Visitors can get a pass to come here and watch people make new laws.

3

The White House

Now we're at the White House. The president of the United States lives and works in the White House. He works in the Oval Office.

4

Oval Office

The White House has 132 rooms. Five of the rooms are open to visitors like us.

5

Pages 4-5:   Ask children to silently read these pages to find out who lives and works at the White House. Ask: *Which part of the text gave you that information? Which part describes the White House?*

Pages 6-7:   Ask: *Which words remind you that the book is being written as a tour?* Have children silently read to find out where George Washington grew up. Have them skim page 7 and share what it tells them about George Washington.

Pages 8-9:   Revisit the contents page. Ask: *How many pages are written about the next topic?* Have children read the pages silently and discuss the pattern used to communicate the information. Have children focus on the Declaration of Independence and discuss why it is side by side with Jefferson's statue.

Pages 10-11:   Establish that these pages describe the Lincoln Memorial. Challenge children to read to find out why the memorial has 36 columns. After viewing the statue, have them think about two words they would use to describe Lincoln.

Pages 12-14:   Have children read these pages independently.

Page 15:   Encourage children to reread page 12 to establish the last place visited. Support them to use the map to answer the question.

Page 16:   Note the index and how to use it.

Have children skim through the chapter headings again to choose which part they would like to read. Give children time to read and review part of the book on their own. Observe how they apply the strategies they used in the first reading. Are they using the contents page effectively? Are they using known words to work out unknown words? Do they understand the information in the written text and photographs?

Rereading and discussing

* Invite responses. Discuss what the children read and the questions they have as a result of the reading.
* Remind children of the strategy used to organize the book. Have them return to the front of the book and skim through the text together, locating the transitions the author used to move the reader from place to place.

Social studies connections

In this activity children will use a map to determine how the places in the capital are related to each other by distance and location.

* Have children open *Our Capital* to pages 14–15. Discuss the information they can learn from the map key. Ask: *What are some things on the map that are not on the map key?*
* Discuss the following questions as they use the map to learn about where the various places in our capital are in relation to each other.

   Which is farther from the White House: the Washington Monument or the Jefferson Memorial?

   What is between the Lincoln Memorial and the Washington Monument?
* Have children make up questions they can answer using the map on these pages.
* Have children use the map to make a flowchart showing the order in which they would visit 5 different places in our capital.

| The White House | → | Washington Monument | → | Bureau of Engraving and Printing | → | National Air and Space Museum |

* Have children share their flowcharts and discuss their reasons for choosing the order that they did.

Reading and writing social studies

* Work with children as they use pages 3–13 to write a paragraph about a visit to the capital.
* Invite children to use the flowchart they made and the frame below to write the sequence paragraph.

   First I visited _____. It was _____. Then I went to see _____. There I saw _____. Next I visited _____. I liked the _____. Then I went to _____. It was _____. Finally, I saw_____. I liked the _____.

Home/school connections

* Encourage children to ask family members if they have ever been to the capital or if they would like to visit it. Tell children to share with their families the names of the places they would like to see if they ever visited the capital and why they would like to see them.
* Invite children to take home the activity sheet from the home/school connections book to do in collaboration with their families.

Anne Miranda

Standards
Culture

Students will learn about their historical roots by reading about the Pilgrims who landed in Plymouth in 1620 and how they can still experience a Pilgrim's life today.

Supports
• photo/text match

Challenges
• proper nouns
• concept of "long, long ago"

Text features
Structure: description

Organization: table of contents, headings

Visual text: passenger list, date on Plymouth Rock

Language: *England, Mayflower, Pilgrims, Plantation, Plymouth, Wampanoag*

Introducing the text
• Have children look at the cover photograph and title. Discuss what they know about Pilgrims. Compare the photo with how most people dress today. Ask children what they think the girl is doing and why. Establish that this happened long, long ago and that the Pilgrims had come to a new land.
• Have children predict what the author might tell about the Pilgrims and how the content will be organized.

The first reading

Contents page: Read and discuss the contents page and photo. Establish that the contents are organized by seasons. Ask: *How does this information match your predictions?*

Pages 2-3: Read the heading and first page. Ask: *What else can you learn from the photograph of the rock?* Have children skim page 3 to find out what problems the Pilgrims had when they arrived.

On September 6, 1620, a group of people called the Pilgrims left England on a ship named the *Mayflower*. They were going to America to start a new life.

It was a long trip. By the time they reached the new land, it was winter and very cold. The Pilgrims had to find a safe place to stop. 3

The First Winter

The Pilgrims made shelters quickly. When a few small houses were built, the Pilgrims moved in.

The first winter in Plymouth was hard because the Pilgrims did not have enough food. The Wampanoag people who lived nearby helped the Pilgrims by giving them food.

6

7

Pages 4-5:   Discuss why page 4 is a painting. Read the passenger list and text and predict the answer to the question on page 5. Ask: *What else does the list tell you?*

Pages 6-7:   Have children read these pages. Ask: *What two problems did the Pilgrims have? How did they solve them?* Discuss strategies for reading and pronouncing *Wampanoag*.

Pages 8-9:   Discuss why the Wampanoag are showing the Pilgrims how to plant the corn. Challenge children to think about how the name *Thanksgiving* was given to the celebration.

Pages 10-15:   Invite children to read these pages independently. Continue to support individuals to glean information from the pictures and written text as needed.

Plymouth Plantation is a living museum. If you go there you can see, hear, smell, taste, and touch things that will help you imagine what life was like for the Pilgrims.

16

Page 16:   Give children time to skim this page before reading it together.

Ask children to share their thoughts about the text. Then encourage them to return to the contents page to choose what they will read independently. Observe how effectively they process the language and monitor their own meaning as they read.

Rereading and discussing

• Encourage children to scan the pictures and to raise questions that were not answered in the text. Support discussion about the questions and ideas for further research.

• Discuss different ways the information in this book could be shared. Share ideas about which methods of presentation might be most effective and why: a time line, a calendar, or a problem/ solution chart.

Social studies connections

In this activity children will fill in a time line to show the events in the order they occurred in the book.

- Discuss the four seasons and the order they were presented in the book.
- List the seasons in order on a time line on chart paper.
- Have children revisit the book to find out which events occurred during each season.
- List children's ideas on the time line.
- Discuss which season would come next if you continued the time line. Establish that they would repeat with *Fall* and that is when we celebrate the first Thanksgiving.

The Pilgrims Come to America

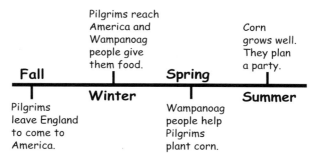

Reading and writing social studies

- Have children revisit page 16. Read the text together and look at the photo.
- Classify a list of things children think they could see, smell, hear, taste, and touch if they visited Plymouth Plantation.
- Have them choose one thing from the list and write a sentence about it. Encourage children to use descriptive words to tell how it might look, smell, sound, taste, or feel.

Home/school connections

- Encourage children to talk with family members about their own Thanksgiving traditions, including looking at photos of family Thanksgiving celebrations if available. Have children share their traditions with the group.
- Invite children to take home the activity sheet from the home/school connections book to do in collaboration with their families.

The Pueblo People

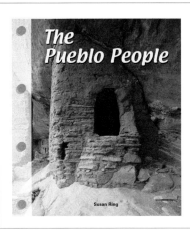

Susan Ring

Standards

Culture

Students will compare their own culture to that of the Pueblo people as they learn about the homes, food, pottery, and traditions of the Pueblo people from the past and present.

Supports
- some repetitive language

Challenges
- variety of sentence structures

Text features

Structure: compare/contrast

Visual text: map, cave paintings

Organization: contents page, headings

Language: proper nouns, present- and past-tense verbs: *live, lived; make, made; use, used; meet, met*

Introducing the text

- Read the title. Establish that the Pueblo people are Native Americans and this is where they lived long ago. Discuss what the cover photo helps tell about them.
- Ask children what they think the author might tell about the Pueblo people. Discuss children's ideas.
- Support children as they read the back-cover blurb. Discuss what information it confirms or adds to their ideas.

The first reading

Contents page: Read the contents page together. Ask: *What will we read about on pages 2 and 3?*

Pages 2-3: Discuss the photographs. Have children silently read the text to find what Pueblo people did long ago that visitors still do today.

The Pueblo People

Do you see the homes in this cliff?
Long ago, the Pueblo people lived here.

2

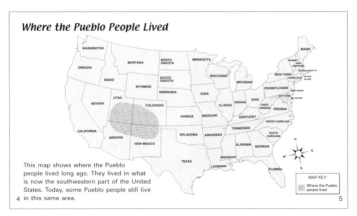

Where the Pueblo People Lived

This map shows where the Pueblo people lived long ago. They lived in what is now the southwestern part of the United States. Today, some Pueblo people still live in this same area.

4

5

Pages 4-5: Support children as they use the map to identify where the Pueblo people lived and where that location is in relation to where the children live.

Pages 6-7: Survey these pages together. Have children look for the pattern the author uses to communicate the information. Have children identify the key words *long ago* and *today* that signal the pattern.

Pages 8-13: Have children read these pages silently to identify the ways the author has compared how Pueblo people lived long ago and how they live today.

Pages 14-15: Ask children to skim these pages to find out how Pueblo people used pictures to tell a story.

Pages 14-16: Invite children to read these pages independently.

Pueblo Traditions

Today, the Pueblo people remember their past in many ways. Sometimes they dress in traditional clothing, like the child you see here. Sometimes they hold special celebrations. These traditions help them to remember their past.

16

Have children return to the contents page to choose which part of the book they will read independently. Observe to what extent they draw on the strategies modeled in the first reading. Are they recognizing and using the pattern of comparing "long ago" and "today" to maintain meaning and momentum?

Rereading and discussing

- Invite responses. Follow the children's lead as you discuss the questions and comments they have about the book. Return to specific pages they talk about. Discuss the literal information communicated through the pictures and text as well as the inferences that can be drawn from them.
- Locate past-tense verbs in the descriptions of "long ago." Encourage children to find the present-tense verb that matches each.

Social studies connections

In this activity children compare and contrast the Pueblo people and their lifestyles from the past with those of the Pueblo people of today.

- Have children open *The Pueblo People* to the contents page. Discuss what the contents page shows they will learn about. Ask: *What do you think you will learn about from the table of contents?*
- Use the table of contents to make a list of topics that are covered.
- Display a graphic organizer to show how to compare and contrast the information in the book.
- Work together with children by skimming through each section that covers the topics you have listed and complete the graphic organizer to show the similarities and differences between the Pueblo people of the past and the present.

Compare and Contrast: Pueblo People Long Ago and Today

Topic	Long Ago	Today
Where they lived	southwestern U.S.	southwestern U.S.
Homes	slept on blankets, met in kiva	live in adobe houses, meet in kiva
Food	ground corn to make cornmeal	grind corn to make cornmeal
Pottery	decorated with red, black, and white patterns and shapes	use the same colors and shapes
Storytelling	painted pictures on walls	tell about the pictures

Reading and writing social studies

- Invite children to revisit their favorite section of the book.
- Discuss how that part of Pueblo life is similar to or different from their own life.
- Have children divide a blank sheet of paper in half and draw a picture of Pueblo life on the left side and a comparable experience from their own life on the right.
- Work together with children to write a sentence for each picture.

Home/school connections

- Encourage children and their families to discuss how their own lives have changed over time, including how their family has grown or changed and how their home has changed.
- Invite children to take home the activity sheet from the home/school connections book to do in collaboration with their families.

Reading Maps

Standards

People, Places, and Environments

Students will draw upon their personal knowledge of photographs of local and distant environments as a basis for exploring different kinds of maps.

Supports

- repetitive pattern of language and information

Challenges

- concept of "perspective"
- comparing photographs with maps

Text features

Structure: compare/contrast

Organization: contents page, headings

Visual text: maps, globe

Language: apostrophe *s*, hyphen: *bird's-eye view*

Introducing the text

- Read the title and discuss the information the cover photo provides. Focus on the size and location of the city, the kinds of buildings, and transportation.
- Have children visualize themselves living in the city in the photograph. Discuss how they would travel to school and what they might do for recreation on weekends.
- Encourage children to think about why we look at maps and photos. Discuss how the information in the photo might look different if it was on a map.

The first reading

Contents page: Read the back-cover blurb together. Then read the contents page to find out what kinds of maps this book tells about. Have children skim the page from top to bottom. Ask: *What pattern of information do you see?* Browse through the book to establish that the maps compare parts of the world progressively from smaller to greater distances. Define *perspective*.

Reading Maps

Contents

David Rhys

Pages 2-3: Compare how the details in these pages are shown. Ask: *What would a map of our classroom look like?*

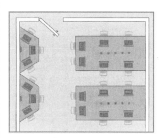

Pages 4-5: Ask: *How has the author made the information easy to understand?* Talk about the structure of the information. Have children read these pages silently.

This is a map of the same classroom. You can see the tables, chairs, and computers. You can see three walls and a door. The only things missing are the children.

3

Pages 6-9: Establish the concept of a "bird's-eye view." Compare details in the photographs and maps.

Pages 10-13: Invite children to scan the photograph on page 10 to find out what information is different from the previous pages. Discuss how this affects the information on the map on page 11. Have children read pages 12 and 13 silently. Encourage them to discuss what they learned.

Pages 14-15: Ask: *What clues help you to know this photo was taken from space? What is the difference between a map and a globe?*

Remember that every map is a picture. It shows a part of our world.

Page 16: Have children read this page independently.

16

Provide time for children to use the contents page to choose and read a few pages independently. Observe their developing strategies. Do they use the organizational features of the book effectively? Do they draw on information shown on each left-hand page to successfully read the facing page? Do they notice detail in photographs and print?

Rereading and discussing

- Support discussion about the children's comments and questions. Ensure that they understand the different information a photo and a map can show.
- Discuss how the structure of the book helps children to read and understand it.
- Encourage children to reread several pages independently or with a friend.

73

Social studies connections

In this activity children will work together to build a model of an imaginary classroom and then draw a bird's-eye-view map of their model.

Materials: building blocks and connecting cubes, posterboard, glue

- Brainstorm a list of items children will include in their model classrooms: chalkboard, desks, chairs, wastebasket, bookshelves.
- Have partners work together to build a model of a classroom by arranging the blocks and cubes on posterboard and then gluing them to their positions.
- Invite partners to then stand above their model and draw a simple bird's-eye-view map of their classroom.
- Collect the maps and have the group work together to match each map with its model.

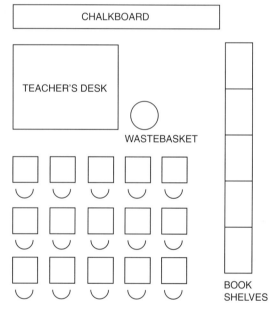

Reading and writing social studies

- Initiate a group discussion about the possible uses for maps. Ask the following questions:

  What can you learn from a map of our city or town?

  When might you need a map?

  How can a map help you?

- Have children write a sentence telling one way maps are helpful.
- Invite children to read their sentences aloud.

Home/school connections

- Encourage children to work together with a family member to draw a map of one room in their home, including labels. Have children bring in their maps to share as others guess which room is represented in each.
- Invite children to take home the activity sheet from the home/school connections book to do in collaboration with their families.

Standards
Science, Technology, and Society

Students will learn the process of shipping goods from nearby and distant places.

Supports
• many high-frequency words

Challenges
• variety of sentence structures
• length of sentences

Text features
Structure: sequence

Organization: table of contents, headings, index

Visual text: map, compass rose, map key

Language: mix of present and past tense

Introducing the text
• Read the title and discuss what *goods* are and where these goods might be coming from. Discuss why people ship goods and include the terms *producers* and *consumers* in the discussion.
• Ask what the word *shipping* means here. Establish that it covers many different ways of getting goods from one place to another.
• Read the back-cover blurb. Have children contribute ideas for a list of goods that come from nearby and another list of goods from far away.

The first reading

Contents page: Draw children's attention to the photo on the contents page. Read the contents. *Note: Although these notes are presented from pages 2–16, each topic is self-contained and the book can be read in any order.*

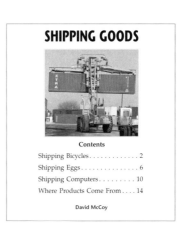

SHIPPING GOODS

Contents

David McCoy

Pages 2-3: Read the heading. Have children skim to find what Jason's question is and what his father told him. Ask: *What word has the author used for the big boxes the bikes are packed in?* Turn to the map on pages 14-15 to identify where Italy is in relation to the United States.

My dad told me that my bike came from Italy. He said that after they made the bikes, they packed them in large metal containers and loaded them on a ship. Then they shipped them across the Atlantic Ocean.

3

Pages 4-5: Ask the group to read these pages silently, then to describe in their own words how the bike got from the ship to the shop. Review the information on pages 2-5 and list each step on a chart.

Pages 6-9: Discuss the information in the photos and written text. Compare and contrast shipping bikes and eggs. Use this information to predict how the computers will be shipped.

Pages 10-13: Have children read these pages silently to find differences in the way these goods are shipped to their final destinations.

Pages 14-15: Read these pages together. Model how to use the map key. Trace the path of the bike from Italy to the United States. Use a globe to show the shortest way for the computers to reach the United States from Japan. Discuss which direction each of the goods is traveling in.

Page 16: Ask: *How do authors organize an index to help you quickly find information?* Practice locating one or two pieces of information.

Invite each child to choose a topic to reread independently. Remind them to keep a list of the steps their product goes through before it reaches the consumer. Observe their reading strategies. Are they able to sustain fluency over the chapter? Do they use a variety of ways to check meaning?

Rereading and discussing

• Support discussion about children's comments and questions. Review pages of their choice. Discuss how *-ed* endings are used to describe events that have already happened.

- Browse through the book together and identify examples of -ed endings on pages 3 and 5.
- Return to the map and practice using the compass rose to describe the shortest route for goods to be shipped to the United States from South America or Africa.

Social studies connections

In this activity children will play a game in which they must order the steps in the process of shipping different goods as presented in the book.

- Have pairs of children choose a product and write on an index card each step involved in the process of shipping that product to a store in the United States.
- Place all of the index cards in a pile facedown on a table.
- Make a chart with headings for each column naming the product.

Bicycles		Eggs		Computers	
Make the bikes	Ship across Atlantic Ocean	Collect eggs	Put in refrigerated truck	Made in factories	Loaded onto trains
Pack in metal containers	Unload boat	Wash eggs	Truck delivers eggs to store	Put on plane or ship	Trains bring computers to towns
Lift containers onto trucks	Trucks drive to town	Conveyor belt puts them into cartons			

- Have children take turns picking a card and placing it in the correct column and then moving cards so that they are in the correct order.
- After all the cards are picked and placed, have the group decide if they are arranged in the correct order. Then glue the cards into place and display the chart on a bulletin board.

Reading and writing social studies

- Set up an appointment with a local grocery store or electronics store manager for children to be present when a delivery is scheduled.
- Have children observe the delivery, then ask the manager questions about where the goods came from and how they got to the store.
- Children can then write about what they learned on their trip.

Home/school connections

- Encourage children to find labels on several items at home that tell where the products were made. Children can then use the map on pages 14–15 to see where their products came from before they were delivered to local stores.
- Invite children to take home the activity sheet from the home/school connections book to do in collaboration with their families.

Standards
Power, Authority, and Governance

Students will learn about civic practices and responsibilities by examining signs and the rules they remind citizens to follow.

Supports
- moderate to strong photo match

Challenges
- elaborated descriptions

Text features
Structure: description

Organization: table of contents, headings

Visual text: signs

Language: *litter, littering, park, parking*

Introducing the text
- Read the title together, then read the information in the back-cover blurb.
- Discuss examples of the kinds of signs mentioned in the back-cover blurb. Reinforce the concept that signs are reminders of rules.
- List the examples as a web and ask children to keep them in mind as they read the book.
- Return to the front-cover picture to talk about where you might see this sign and what it tells you.

The first reading

Contents page: Skim the table of contents. Ask: *Where will we begin to read about danger? What are some of the signs you see that warn you of danger?*

Now the sign tells people it is not safe to cross the street.

Pages 2-3: Read the information in the street signs. Have children scan the text to find the words that describe the purpose of these signs.

Pages 4-5: Read the heading and discuss what the children think the word *littering* means. Have them read silently to find what would happen if people were allowed to litter.

Pages 6-9: Discuss the signs and compare the amount of information in them. Ask: *What do people have to know to understand the thin ice sign? the no swimming sign? the stop sign? the railway crossing sign? Why do some signs have pictures as well as writing?*

Pages 10-11: Invite children to read and find why these two signs are important. Ask: *Which words tell who each sign helps? Which words tell how each sign helps?*

Pages 12-15: Challenge children to look at each sign and predict what the written text will tell them before reading and checking or self-correcting their prediction.

Page 16: Have children read this page independently. Discuss the possible consequences of not obeying the zoo signs. Ask: *What is one way these signs could have been written using just one word?*

Zoo Signs

DO NOT FEED
THE ANIMALS

DO NOT FEED

Why do you think these signs are important?

16

When you are confident that children have enough information, ask them to read several pages of the book aloud independently.

Invite children to use the contents page to choose which part of the text they will reread. Have them set a purpose and keep this purpose in their head as they read. Observe their strategies and behaviors. Do they self-correct close to the point of error? Do they use known words and parts of words to work out unfamiliar vocabulary? Are they enjoying what they read?

Rereading and discussing

• Have children share their responses and questions about their favorite pages with a buddy.
• Follow children's leads to determine a focus for further discussion.
• Work together with the group to redesign one of the signs.

Social studies connections

In this activity children will explore signs that relate to their own lives.

- Create a sign checklist by labeling three columns on a chart with the following headings:

  Sign   **Observed**   **Where**
- Revisit the book as you work together with the group to list the signs presented in the first column.
- Take the group on a walk around the neighborhood and the school.
- Have pairs of children work on a checklist together by checking each sign they observe and writing where they see it.
- Work with children to list any additional signs they see on their walk.
- Upon returning to the classroom, have partners share and compare checklists.

Sign	Observed	Where
Walk/Don't Walk	✓	On the corner near school
No Littering	✓	On Main Street
No Swimming		
Danger, Thin Ice		
Stop	✓	On Park Avenue
Railway Crossing		
Saving Parking Space	✓	In the school parking lot
Priority Seating		
Road Signs	✓	In front of the school
Zoo Signs		
Exit	✓	Above the hallway door
Slippery When Wet	✓	On the bridge
No Running	✓	On the school bus

Reading and writing social studies

- Discuss with children some of the rules they should follow in the classroom.
- Have each group member design a sign to be displayed in the classroom for one of the rules you have discussed.
- Children may wish to design signs for rules such as: *No Talking, Raise Your Hand to Speak, No Running, Read Silently.*
- Remind children to include the words and a picture that best represents each rule.

Home/school connections

- Encourage children to take a walk around their own neighborhood with a family member to look for local signs. Have children keep a list of the signs they see and share it with the group.
- Invite children to take home the activity sheet from the home/school connections book to do in collaboration with their families.

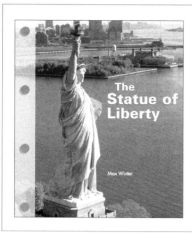

Standards
Civic Ideals and Practices

Students will learn about the significance of the Statue of Liberty and the obstacles that were overcome in transporting and displaying it.

Supports
- photo/text match
- easily decodable words

Challenges
- proper nouns
- concept of "symbol"

Text features
Structure: problem/solution

Organization: table of contents, headings

Language: *symbol, liberty, freedom, Frédéric Bartholdi, pedestal*

Introducing the text
- Read the title. Talk about the cover photo and establish that the statue is a symbol of freedom and what this means.
- Read the back-cover blurb and through further discussion link the concepts of "liberty" and "freedom."
- Discuss other familiar national and local symbols the children know, such as the U.S. flag and their state flag.

The first reading
Contents page: Skim the table of contents together. Encourage children to think of a question each entry might raise or answer.

Lady Liberty

This is the Statue of Liberty. She is often called Lady Liberty. She stands in the harbor of New York City.

The French people gave the statue to the American people as a sign of friendship and a symbol of liberty. Liberty means freedom.

Pages 2-3:	Match the heading and its table of contents entry. Ask: *What is the purpose of a heading?* Confirm that a heading tells what we will read about. Have the children read silently to find where the statue stands. Discuss why they think this place was chosen.

The man who created the drawing was Frédéric Bartholdi. He also directed the building of the statue.

5

Pages 4-5: Guide the children to read these pages independently for the most part. Share strategies for pronouncing Frédéric Bartholdi's name.

Pages 6-7: Encourage children to think about the list of information the author is providing. Review this list. Ask: *What problem might the French have when the statue has to be shipped to the United States? What are some ways they could solve that problem?*

Pages 8-9: Have children read silently to find how the first problem was overcome and what the next problem was. Ask: *What is a pedestal? What it is used for?* Discuss the clues the author gave to help them know this.

Pages 10-11: Continue to support independent reading.

Pages 12-15: Compare the two celebrations for Lady Liberty.

Page 16: After reading the heading together, have children read this page independently.

Visiting Lady Liberty

Today, people from all over the world come to see the statue. These children climbed up the stairs inside Lady Liberty. They went all the way up to her crown!

16

Give children time to reread and review interesting parts of the book together. Observe how effectively they use the table of contents and headings. Are they monitoring meaning closely as they read?

Rereading and discussing

- Invite personal responses to the information in the book. What did the children learn? What did the book make them think about?
- Browse through the book together to discuss problems and solutions. Encourage children to suggest different solutions. Think of and share different ways to record the information using graphic organizers.

Social studies connections

In this activity children will explore the relationship between problems and solutions, and then use what they discover to create graphic organizers that show the problems and solutions presented in the book.

- Lead a discussion to encourage children to share problems they have solved in their own lives.
- Ask the following questions to help children think of problems and solutions:

  Did you ever have to move something that was too heavy? What did you do to move it?

  Were you ever too small to see a show or a play? What did you do so that you could see it?

- List children's responses in a problem/solution graphic organizer.
- Display 2 problem/solution graphic organizers on the chalkboard.
- Work together with children to complete the two main problems that were solved in *The Statue of Liberty*.

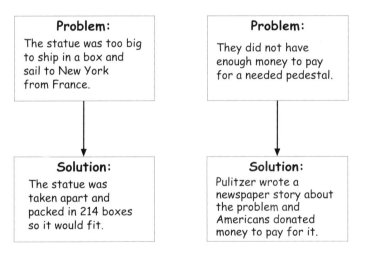

Problem:	**Problem:**
The statue was too big to ship in a box and sail to New York from France.	They did not have enough money to pay for a needed pedestal.

Solution:	**Solution:**
The statue was taken apart and packed in 214 boxes so it would fit.	Pulitzer wrote a newspaper story about the problem and Americans donated money to pay for it.

Reading and writing social studies

- Revisit pages 2 and 3 in the book. Reread the text and scan the photograph.
- Have children share what they feel when they hear the words *friendship* and *freedom*.
- Have children choose one of the words and draw a picture to show what it means to them.
- Support children to write a sentence about their pictures.

Home/school connections

- Encourage children and their families to visit a statue or other memorial in their town. Have children share what they saw and learned after their visit.
- Invite children to take home the activity sheet from the home/school connections book to do in collaboration with their families.

Meish Goldish

Standards
Civic Ideals and Practices

Students will develop an understanding of the importance of trees and learn how people continue to help renew these essential natural resources.

Supports
- large percentage of high-frequency words
- strong photo support

Challenges
- maintaining meaning over continuous text
- variety of sentence structures

Text features
Structure: cause and effect

Organization: table of contents, headings

Visual text: inset

Language: suffixes: *-ing, -s, 's, -ed*

Introducing the text
- Discuss the title and cover picture. Draw on children's prior knowledge to build a web listing how trees help us.
- Ask children to refer to the web and add details as they read the book.
- Use the web to predict what the author might write about trees.

The first reading
Contents page: Read the contents page. Compare it to ideas on the web. Use the contents page to locate, browse, and discuss the content of specific entries.

Pages 2–3: Ask the group to read these pages silently to find why trees are an important natural resource.

Trees make our neighborhoods beautiful, and they give us shade on sunny days.

2

But do you know all the other ways that trees help us? Trees are an important natural resource. They help us in many ways.

3

Pages 4-5: Explain that this text has a cause-and-effect structure. Help identify the information communicated on these pages using this structure. Draw and label two columns *Cause* and *Effect*. Record the information in each column.

Some trees give us fruit. Apples, oranges, pears, plums, and cherries grow on trees.
6   Fruit is delicious and good for you.

Pages 6-9: Continue to support largely independent reading of these pages and record the information.

Pages 10-11: Read the heading together. Ask children to silently read page 10, then reread it and make a list in their head of the information the author has provided. Share their lists. Ask children to keep a list in their head as they read page 11. Share what they did to help remember their lists.

Pages 12-15: Read the heading and browse through the information together. Ask: *Why did J. Sterling Morton want people to plant trees? Why should children plant a tree where they live?*

Trees and the Future

It takes many years for a tree to grow. Planting new trees means that people will always have trees to use and enjoy in the future.

16

Page 16: Invite children to read this page independently.

Give children time to read and review the book independently. Observe how they use the table of contents to choose what they will read.

Rereading and discussing

- Have children reflect on the information by asking them what they learned, what their questions are now, and how trees help their neighborhood.
- Explore the cause-and-effect structure of the book and add information to the table.
- Have children choose two pages to read with a buddy.

Social studies connections

In this activity children will explore the importance of trees in their local environment.

- Revisit the book and work with children to create a checklist of the different ways trees help us.
- Have each student copy the checklist and take it with them on a trip to a local park or neighborhood that has many trees.
- Work together to observe local trees and complete the checklists.

How Trees In Our Neighborhood Help Us	Yes	No
Make neighborhood beautiful	✓	
Give us shade	✓	
Keep air fresh and clean	✓	
Roots keep soil from washing away	✓	
Give fruit	✓	
Birds live in nests		✓
Have acorns		✓

Reading and writing social studies

- Talk with children about different ways they could celebrate Arbor Day. Have them draw a picture and write a sentence to show their favorite way.

Home/school connections

- Invite children to discuss the importance of trees with family members and take a vote on which kind of tree they would like to choose as their "Favorite Family Tree." Encourage children to look in books, magazines, or other resources to find a picture of their "Family Tree" and share it with the group.
- Invite children to take home the activity sheet from the home/school connections book to do in collaboration with their families.

Volunteers

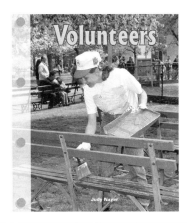

Standards

Civic Ideals and Practices

Students will be introduced to civic ideals and practices by learning about the various ways volunteers help our communities.

Supports
- photo/text match
- consistent pattern of information

Challenges
- elaborated events

Text features

Structure: question and answer

Organization: table of contents, headings

Language: *helping, reading, painting, planting, checking*

Introducing the text

- Read to find out if the title or the back-cover blurb tells what volunteers are and what they do. Discuss the information and check it against the contents page.
- Record the information as a web. Tell the group that the introduction could provide further information. Ask them to silently read page 2. Add the definition of *volunteers* to the web.

The first reading

Contents page: Return to the contents page and suggest reading *How Do Volunteers Help the Community?* first.

Pages 2-3: Recall the information on page 2 before reading the heading on page 3. Speculate on ways volunteers might help in a community and how the volunteers in the photograph are helping. Have children silently read, then share what they find out.

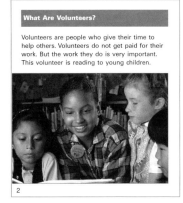

What Are Volunteers?

Volunteers are people who give their time to help others. Volunteers do not get paid for their work. But the work they do is very important. This volunteer is reading to young children.

2

Pages 4-6:	Ask children to skim these pages to find out why and how volunteers are helping. Add the information to the web.
Pages 7-9:	Read the question together. Ask children to survey the pages to discover which examples the author has used before recording it on the web.

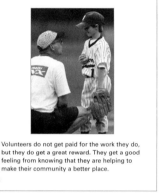

How Do Volunteers Help the Environment?

Many volunteers work to help the environment. These volunteers are planting a tree. People need trees because trees make the oxygen that we need to breathe. 7

Pages 10-15:	Return to the contents page to check the topics of these pages. Invite each child to choose one topic to read silently. Then have them share how the volunteers were helping. Add the information to the web.
Page 16:	Read this page together.

Volunteers do not get paid for the work they do, but they do get a great reward. They get a good feeling from knowing that they are helping to make their community a better place.

16

Give children time to reread and review part of the book independently or with a buddy. Observe what interests them, how they go about problem-solving, and how they use the contents page and headings.

Rereading and discussing

- Choose one entry and discuss the pattern the author has used to write about each set of volunteers. Invite children to reread another entry independently, keeping the pattern in mind. Discuss how this helps them to predict and maintain meaning.
- Have children name a volunteer in your community. Brainstorm how that person helps. Use the web to record the information. Use the author's pattern to compare and write the information.
- Scan the book together to find the words used to describe how volunteers helped. Discuss why these words end in *-ing* and suggest other words that could have been used.

Social studies connections

In this activity children will generate questions about volunteers and use research and study skills to locate and write the answers.

Materials: 3 index cards for each group member

- Have children use the book as a reference to help them brainstorm a list of questions about volunteers.
- Keep the list of questions displayed as each child chooses 3 questions to write on individual index cards.
- Have children then find and write the answer to each question they chose on the back of their index cards.
- Children can then read and try to answer each other's questions. They can confirm answers by reading the back of the index card.

Front of index card	Back of index card
How do volunteers help the environment?	planting trees, cleaning up a field, sorting trash

Reading and writing social studies

- Take children on a trip to a local hospital, fire station, library, or other place in the community where they can see and talk to volunteers.
- Have children ask the volunteers they meet any questions they might have.
- Children can then draw a picture to show one thing they learned from the volunteers they talked to and write a sentence to go with it.

Home/school connections

- Encourage children to volunteer their services in their own home. Suggest things like volunteering to walk a pet, clear the table, or clean up their yard. Have children then report back to the group about their experience.
- Invite children to take home the activity sheet from the home/school connections book to do in collaboration with their families.

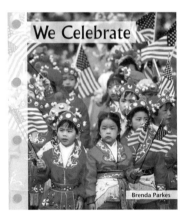

Standards

Individual Development and Identity

Students will explore cultural diversity by learning about traditional celebrations from six different heritages that are represented in America.

Supports

- appealing topic
- repetitive pattern of information

Challenges

- proper nouns – *Tulip Festival, West Indian, Puerto Rican, Cinco de Mayo*
- concept of "cultures"

Text features

Structure: description

Organization: table of contents, headings, labels

Language: *celebrate, celebration, festivals, parades, heritage*

Introducing the text

- Read the title and focus discussion on the front cover and what the people are doing. Write *Celebrate* on chart paper and have children help write *Celebrating*. Ask children why people celebrate, then discuss what the people in the photo might be celebrating.
- Discuss what being *proud of something* means.
- Check the back-cover blurb to see what information it has. List some cultural celebrations the group knows about and the special events that happen at these celebrations.

The first reading

Contents page: Compare the table of contents with the list.

We come from many different countries, but we are all Americans. We are proud of our many cultures.

2

On special days each year, we celebrate our cultures with festivals and parades.

3

Pages 2-3:   Ask: *What three things are the children telling you on page 2?* Discuss these. Have children look on page 3 to find how the children celebrate their cultures. Turn back to the contents page to see which celebration you will read about on page 4.

Pages 4-5:   Challenge children to read the heading and find what the children are given to honor the new year. Ask: *Why do you think the lion dance is part of the parade?* Point out the label on the photo on page 5. Ask: *What does the label tell you?*

Pages 6-7:   Read the heading. Establish that it tells when the celebration is held (May 5). Have children skim to find how people celebrate their Mexican heritage. Share strategies for reading *mariachi.* After reading these pages ask: *How were pages 4-5 the same as pages 6-7?* Read the label together.

San Francisco, California

We also have a big parade. The lion dance is my favorite part of the parade. The lion dance brings happiness and good fortune.

5

Pages 8-9:   Ask: *How are these pages the same as pages 4-7?* Challenge children to use the pattern of information to help them silently read these pages. Discuss how the *klompen* dancers got their name.

Pages 10-13:   Continue checking print and pictures for information.

Pages 14-15:   Read the heading. Ask: *How are these people celebrating their culture?* Establish what a carnival is, what the people are wearing, and what the words *island nations* mean.

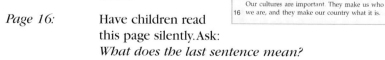

Our cultures are important. They make us who we are, and they make our country what it is.

16

Page 16:   Have children read this page silently. Ask: *What does the last sentence mean?*

Provide time for children to reread and review their book. Observe their strategies. Are they using the pattern of information to maintain forward momentum? Are they rereading to check and confirm or self-correct? Are they drawing on detail in pictures and print in an integrated way?

Rereading and discussing

- Share children's responses. Discuss what celebrations they would like to see and why. Have them share questions they have.
- Set a purpose for rereading by inviting children to think about the similarities and differences among the cultural celebrations.
- Invite children to choose one celebration to reread with a buddy.

Social studies connections

In this activity children use word webs to organize the information they have learned about the various celebrations.

- Model making a word web for the first celebration presented in the book: Chinese New Year.

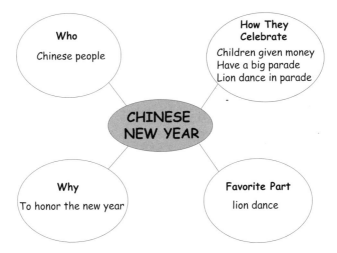

- Encourage children to help identify headings for each part of the web.
- Work together with the group to complete the web.
- Have children then work to create a word web for three other celebrations by assigning one celebration to each pair.
- Provide time for the group to share their webs and add one more topic to each, such as **Favorite Part**.

Reading and writing social studies

- List the following United States holidays on the chalkboard and discuss what each is with the group: Thanksgiving, Independence Day, Valentine's Day, New Year's Day.
- Invite children to choose one holiday, then draw a picture and write a sentence to show and tell one way they celebrate that holiday.

Home/school connections

- Encourage children to ask family members what their favorite family celebration is and why. Invite them to share any photos they may have of the celebration.
- Invite children to take home the activity sheet from the home/school connections book to do in collaboration with their families.

We Vote

Cynthia Martin

Standards
Civic Ideals and Practices

Students will learn how people use the right to vote to create and change structures of power and authority.

Supports
• many high-frequency words

Challenges
• some concepts
• interpreting chart

Text features

Structure: problem/solution

Visual text: chart

Organization: table of contents, headings, glossary

Language: bolded words

Introducing the text

• Tell children that the book describes some different things people vote for and different ways of voting. Have them recall times when they have voted. Ask them to tell why they voted and how they voted. Have children share reasons they think voting might be important.

• Discuss the front-cover picture before reading the back-cover blurb.

The first reading

Contents page: Browse through the contents page. Select one or two topics, then locate them and skim the pictures to get an idea of the information. Note and talk about the role of a glossary.

Pages 2-3: Discuss the information in the pictures and chart. Ask: *What information does each give you about voting?* Have children read to find out why the children were voting and what the outcome was.

Our Field Trip		
Zoo	🐾	⊮⊬
Children's Museum	🦘	IIII
Aquarium	🐬	⊮⊬ III

This chart shows how the children voted. Votes were counted by making **tally marks**. Each child voted for one place. Each vote got a mark like this: I.

This shows four votes: IIII. This shows five votes: ⊮⊬.

Most of the **voters** chose the aquarium.

3

Pages 4-5:   Ask: *What does the heading tell you to expect to read about? How are these adults voting?* Have children predict what a *ballot* is before checking the definition in the glossary.

How Adults Vote

Adults vote too. Sometimes people vote by marking a paper called a **ballot**. Then the votes
4 on all the ballots are counted.

Pages 6-9:   Return to the contents page. Have half the group find and silently read *Voting About Safety* and the other half read *Voting About Money*. Have each group share what they learned.

Pages 10-13:   Continue to support reading and discussion of these pages. Encourage children to try to define bolded text in their own words before checking the glossary definition.

Glossary

ballot: a piece of paper that shows a secret vote

community: a group of people living and working together in the same place

leaders: people who represent larger groups of people in communities

president: the person at the head of a group, community, or country

tally marks: lines used to record and count the number of things in a group

vice president: the person who is next in command after a president

vote: a way a person can show his or her choice

voters: people who vote

voting machine: a machine that counts votes

16

Pages 14-15:   Read these pages and establish that the purpose of voting is to help make choices fairly.

Page 16:   Have students recall the role and importance of a glossary.

Provide time for children to return to the contents page to choose an entry to read independently. Observe how effectively they utilize the contents page, headings, and glossary.

Rereading and discussing

- Review children's personal responses to the book and revisit pages that are particularly interesting to them.
- Explain that the text has a problem/solution structure. Browse through the book together and identify problems and solutions. Explore different ways graphic organizers could be used to communicate the information.
- Invite children to choose another entry from the table of contents to read with a buddy.

Social studies connections

In this activity children experience participating in and analyzing the voting process.

- Have children revisit page 3 of the book. Discuss the headings and entries on the chart.
- Brainstorm a list of ideas the group would like to have a vote about. Display the list on the board.
- Work together with the group to create a chart they can use to record their votes. Encourage children to tell what headings and entries to include in the chart.
- Have children then vote, record, and analyze the results.
- Provide time for the group to work on their own to make charts, vote, and record the results for the other voting ideas they suggested.

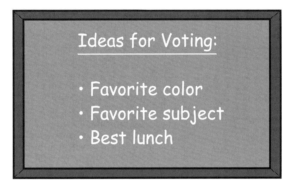

Ideas for Voting:

- Favorite color
- Favorite subject
- Best lunch

Favorite Color	
Red	||
Blue	|||
Green		

Reading and writing social studies

- Work with children as they use the results of one of their voting charts to write a paragraph summarizing the results.
- Invite children to use the frame below to help them write their summaries.

  Today we voted on _____. The _____ that got the most votes was _____. The _____ with the least votes was _____.

Home/school connections

- Encourage children to conduct a vote with family members to determine their favorite family activity. Have children share the voting results with the group.
- Invite children to take home the activity sheet from the home/school connections book to do in collaboration with their families.

Standards/Benchmarks

Title	Standards
A City Grows	● Time, Continuity, and Change ▲ Environment and Society
Coming to America	● Global Connections ▲ The World in Spatial Terms
Communities	● Individuals, Groups, and Institutions ▲ Places and Regions
Going West	● Individuals, Groups, and Institutions ▲ Human Systems
Good Neighbors	● Global Connections ▲ The World in Spatial Terms ▲ Places and Regions
How Paper Is Made	● Science, Technology, and Society ▲ Environment and Society ▲ Human Systems
Keeping Bees	● Production, Distribution, and Consumption ▲ Environment and Society
Landforms	● People, Places, and Environments ▲ Places and Regions ▲ Physical Systems
Looking at Money	● Power, Authority, and Governance
Making Choices	● Production, Distribution, and Consumption ▲ Environment and Society
Maybe I Could	● Individual Development and Identity ▲ Environment and Society
National Parks	● People, Places, and Environments ▲ Places and Regions ▲ Physical Systems

● National Council of Social Studies (NCSS) Standards
▲ National Geography Standards, K–4

Benchmarks

Knows how areas of a community have changed over time in terms of size and style of homes; how people earn their living; changes in plant and animal population.

Understands the changes that occur in people's lives when they move from faraway places to the United States.

Knows similarities and differences in house and land use in urban and suburban areas.

Understands what life was like for children and families "on the trail," when they moved from one part of the United States to another.

Knows the locations of home, school, neighborhood, community, state, and country.

Knows that capital resources are things made by people and are used to make their goods or to provide services.

Knows that most people work in jobs where they produce a few special goods or services.

Knows that places can be defined in terms of their dominant human and physical characteristics.

Understands the contributions and significance of historical figures in the community.

Knows that opportunity cost is what someone gives up in order to get something; and that when someone chooses to buy goods or services, there is always an opportunity cost.

Understands broad categories of time (today and in the future).

Knows the ways people take aspects of the environment into account when deciding on locations for human activities.

From *CONTENT KNOWLEDGE: A Compendium of Standards and Benchmarks for K-12 Education,* written by John S. Kendall and Robert J. Marzano. Copyright ©1996 by Mid-Continent Regional Educational Laboratory, Inc.

Title	Standards
The Olympics	● Time, Continuity, and Change
Our Capital	● Power, Authority, and Governance ▲ The World in Spatial Terms
The Pilgrims	● Culture ▲ The Uses of Geography ▲ Places and Regions
The Pueblo People	● Culture ▲ Human Systems
Reading Maps	● People, Places, and Environments ▲ The World in Spatial Terms
Shipping Goods	● Science, Technology, and Society ▲ Human Systems ▲ Environment and Society
Signs	● Power, Authority, and Governance
The Statue of Liberty	● Civic Ideals and Practices
Taking Care of Trees	● Civic Ideals and Practices ▲ Environment and Society
Volunteers	● Civic Ideals and Practices
We Celebrate	● Individual Development and Identity
We Vote	● Civic Ideals and Practices

● National Council of Social Studies (NCSS) Standards
▲ National Geography Standards, K-4

Benchmarks

Understands cultural heritage through stories, songs, and celebrations.

Knows why important buildings, statues, and monuments are associated with state and national history.

Knows ways in which early explorers and settlers adapted to, used, and changed the environment of the state or region.

Understands through legends, myths, and archaeological evidence the origins and culture of early Native Americans or Hawaiians who lived in the state or region.

Knows major physical and human features of places as they are represented on maps and globes.

Knows the modes of transportation used to move people, products, and ideas from place to place, their importance, and their advantages and disadvantages.

Understands why civic responsibility is important, and knows examples of civic responsibility.

Knows the history of the American symbols (e.g., the eagle, the Liberty Bell, George Washington as "The Father of Our Country," the national flag).

Knows how human activities have increased the ability of the physical environment to support human life in the local community, state, United States, and other countries.

Knows ways that people solve common problems by cooperating.

Understands personal or cultural heritage through stories, songs, and celebrations.

Knows that procedural justice refers to problems arising over fair ways to gather information and make just decisions; knows examples of situations involving procedural justice.

From *CONTENT KNOWLEDGE: A Compendium of Standards and Benchmarks for K-12 Education*, written by John S. Kendall and Robert J. Marzano. Copyright © 1996 by Mid-Continent Regional Educational Laboratory, Inc.

Bibliography

A City Grows Documents events in the history of Chicago.

Fiction
- *The Little House* by Virginia Lee Burton (Houghton Mifflin, 1978)
- *Sara's City* by Sue Alexander (Houghton Mifflin, 1995)

Non-Fiction
- *Chicago, Illinois* by Mary Turck (Crestwood, 1989)
- *Cities* ed. by Alan Fallow (Time-Life, 1994)
- *The Sears Tower* by Craig A. Doherty (Blackbirch, 1995)

Coming to America Explores the experience of immigrants at Ellis Island in the early twentieth century.

Fiction
- *My Grandmother's Journey* by John Cech (Bradbury, 1991)
- *When Jessie Came Across the Sea* by Amy Hest (Candlewick, 1997)

Non-Fiction
- *Grandfather's Journey* by Allen Say (Houghton Mifflin, 1993)
- *Where Did Your Family Come From?* by Melvin Berger and Gilda Berger (Ideals, 1993)

Communities Helps children learn about the ways people in urban, suburban, and rural communities live.

Fiction
- *One Afternoon* by Yumi Heo (Orchard, 1994)
- *The Town Mouse & the Country Mouse* adapted by Janet Stevens (Holiday House, 1987)

Non-Fiction
- *A City Album* by P. Roop & C. Roop (Heinemann, 1998)
- *Town and Country* by Alice and Martin Provensen (Harcourt Brace, 1991)

Going West Focuses on the way people traveled across the country long ago and the hardships they overcame to reach their destinations.

Fiction
- *Prairie Day* adapted by Laura Ingalls Wilder (HarperCollins, 1997)
- *Wagons West!* by Roy Gerrard (Farrar, Straus & Giroux, 1996)
- *Wagon Wheels* by Barbara Brenner (HarperCollins, 1993)

Non-Fiction
- *If You Traveled West in a Covered Wagon* by Ellen Levine (Scholastic, 1991)
- *Kids in Pioneer Times* by Lisa A. Wroble (Rosen, 1997)

Good Neighbors Two children share information about their different countries.

Fiction
- *Chave's Memories* by Maria I. Delgado (Arte Publico, 1996)
- *Dear Annie* by Judith Caseley (Greenwillow, 1991)
- *Kate on the Coast* by Pat Brisson (Simon & Schuster, 1992)

Non-Fiction
- *Canada* by Elaine Landau (Children's Press, 2000)
- *Mexico* by Helen Arnold (Raintree Steck-Vaughn, 1996)
- *The Piñata Maker* by George Ancona (Harcourt Brace, 1994)

How Paper Is Made Shows the process by which wood is manufactured into paper.

Fiction
- *Paper Bird* by Arcadio Lobato (Carolrhoda, 1993)
- *The Paper Princess* by Elisa Klevens (Dutton, 1994)

Non-Fiction
- *How Is Paper Made?* by Isaac Asimov & Elizabeth Kaplan (Gareth Stevens, 1993)
- *Paper, Paper Everywhere* by Gail Gibbons (Harcourt Brace, 1997)

Keeping Bees Describes how people keep bees to produce honey and beeswax.

Fiction
- *The Bee Tree* by Patricia Polacco (Putnam, 1998)

Non-Fiction
- *The Bee* by Sabrina Crewe (Raintree Steck-Vaughn, 1997)
- *The Honey Makers* by Gail Gibbons (William Morrow, 1997)
- *The Magic School Bus Inside a Beehive* by Joanna Cole (Scholastic, 1996)

Landforms Names and pictures bodies of water and land.

Fiction
- *The Earth and I* by Frank Asch (Harcourt Brace, 1994)
- *Listen to the Desert* by Pat Mora (Clarion, 1994)
- *My River* by Shari Halpern (Simon & Schuster, 1992)

Non-Fiction
- *America the Beautiful* by Kathleen Lee Bates (Athcneum, 1993)
- *How Mountains Are Made* by Kathleen W. Zoehfeld (HarperCollins, 1995)

Looking at Money Relates the background of historical figures pictured on American currency.

Fiction
* *Bunny Money* by Rosemary Wells (HarperCollins, 1997)
* *Jelly Beans for Sale* by Bruce McMillan (Scholastic, 1996)

Non-Fiction
* *The Go-Around Dollar* by Barbara J. Adams (Simon & Schuster, 1992)
* *The Story of Money* by Betsy Maestro (Clarion, 1993)

Making Choices Explores factors involved in making everyday decisions and the opportunity cost of each choice.

Fiction
* *Henry and Mudge and Annie's Perfect Pet* by Cynthia Rylant (Simon & Schuster, 1999)
* *Pick a Pet* by Shelley Rotner and Cheo García (Orchard, 1999)

Maybe I Could Encourages thinking about pursuing a career based upon present interests.

Fiction
* *I Want to Be* by Thylias Moss (Dial, 1993)
* *I Want to Be an Astronaut* by Byron Barton (HarperCollins, 1988)
* *If I Could Work* by Terrence Blacker (J. B. Lippincott, 1987)

Non-Fiction
* *A Day in the Life of a Teacher* by Mary Bowman-Kruhm (Rosen, 1999)
* *Here Comes Mr. Eventoff with the Mail* by Alice Flanagan (Children's Press, 1998)
* *I'm Going to Be a Police Officer* by Edith Kunhardt (Scholastic, 1995)
* *Jobs People Do* by Christopher Maynard (DK Publishing, 1997)

National Parks Explains what national parks are, where they are, what they offer us, and why their preservation is important.

Fiction
* *One Blowy Night* by Nick Butterworth (Little, Brown, 1992)
* *When I Go Camping with Grandma* by Marion Dane Bauer (Bridgewater, 1995)

Non-Fiction
* *America's Top 10 National Parks* by Jenny Tesar (Blackbirch, 1998)
* *A Child's Glacier Bay* by Kimberley Corral with Hannah Corral (Graphic Arts Center, 1998)
* *Yellowstone ABC* by Cyd Martin Roberts (Rinehart, 1992)

The Olympics Details the history behind the tradition of the Olympic Games as they are held in modern times.

Fiction
* *D.W. Flips!* by Marc Brown (Little, Brown, 1997)
* *Hour of the Olympics* by Mary Pope Osborne (Random House, 1998)

Non-Fiction
* *A Picture Book of Jesse Owens* by David A. Adler (Holiday House, 1992)
* *Wilma Unlimited: How Wilma Rudolph Became the World's Fastest Woman* by Kathleen Krull (Harcourt Brace, 1996)

Our Capital Conducts children on a mini-tour of monuments, museums, and other sights in Washington, D.C.

Fiction
* *A Big Cheese for the White House* by Candace Fleming (DK Publishing, 1999)
* *Woodrow, the White House Mouse* by Peter W. Barnes (Scholastic, 1998)

Non-Fiction
* *The Story of the White House* by K. Waters (Scholastic, 1991)
* *A Visit to Washington, D.C.* by Jill Krementz (Scholastic, 1989)
* *Washington, D.C.: A Scrapbook* by Laura Lee Benson (Charlesbridge, 1999)

The Pilgrims Relates the story of the Pilgrims' journey from England and how they survived their first year.

Fiction
* *Molly's Pilgrim* by Barbara Cohen (Bantam Doubleday Dell, 1983)
* *Three Young Pilgrims* by Cheryl Harness (Macmillan, 1992)

Non-Fiction
* *The First Thanksgiving* by Jean Craighead George (Philomel, 1993)
* *Tapenum's Day: A Wampanoag Indian Boy in Pilgrim Times* by Kate Waters (Scholastic, 1996)

The Pueblo People Tells about the lifestyle, traditions, and legacy of the Pueblo people of the Southwest.

Fiction
* *Coyote: A Trickster Tale from the American Southwest* by Gerald McDermott (Harcourt Brace, 1994)
* *Crow and Hawk* retold by M. Rosen (Harcourt Brace, 1995)

Non-Fiction
* *Dancing Rainbows: A Pueblo Boy's Story* by Evelyn Clarke Mott (Cobblehill, 1996)
* *Earth Daughter: Alicia of Acoma Pueblo* by George Ancona (Simon & Schuster, 1995)

Reading Maps Introduces children to the concept of maps as pictures of their world from near and far away.

Fiction
- *Are We There Yet, Daddy?* by Virginia Walters (Viking, 1999)
- *My Map Book* by Sara Finelli (HarperCollins, 1995)

Non-Fiction
- *Me on the Map* by Joan Sweeney (Crown, 1996)
- *The Whole World in Your Hands: Looking at Maps* by Melvin Berger and Gilda Berger (Ideals, 1993)

Shipping Goods Helps children understand that goods are moved from where they are made to where they are sold.

Fiction
- *Big City Port* by Betsy Maestro (Macmillan, 1994)
- *How to Make an Apple Pie and See the World* by Marjorie Priceman (Alfred A. Knopf, 1994)
- *The Tortilla Factory* by G. Paulsen (Harcourt Brace, 1995)

Non-Fiction
- *Extra Cheese, Please: Mozzarella's Journey from Cow to Pizza* by Cris Peterson (Boyds Mills, 1994)
- *Inside a Freight Train* by E. J. McHenry (Cobblehill, 1993)

Signs Explains how signs help people by giving them important information.

Fiction
- *I See a Sign* by Lars Klove (Simon & Schuster, 1996)
- *Red Light, Green Light* by Margaret Wise Brown (Scholastic, 1994)

Non-Fiction
- *Puff...Flash...Bang: A Book About Signals* by Gail Gibbons (William Morrow, 1993)
- *Signs* by Ron and Nancy Goor (HarperCollins, 1983)

The Statue of Liberty Details the story behind "Lady Liberty," a gift from France that became a symbol of America.

Fiction
- *How the Second Grade Raised $8,205.50 to Visit the Statue of Liberty* by Nathan Zimelman (Albert Whitman, 1992)
- *Watch the Stars Come Out* by Riki Levinson (Dutton, 1985)

Non-Fiction
- *If Your Name Was Changed at Ellis Island* by Ellen Levine (Scholastic, 1994)
- *Our National Symbols* by Linda Carlson Johnson (Millbrook, 1992)
- *The Statue of Liberty* by Lucille Recht Penner (Random House, 1995)

Taking Care of Trees Focuses on trees as a natural resource that must be protected by all responsible citizens.

Fiction
* *The Apple Pie Tree* by Zoe Hall (Scholastic, 1996)
* *The Giving Tree* by Shel Silverstein (HarperCollins, 1994)
* *Someday a Tree* by Eve Bunting (Houghton Mifflin, 1996)
* *A Tree for Me* by Nancy Van Laan (Alfred A. Knopf, 2000)

Non-Fiction
* *Be a Friend to Trees* by Patricia Lauber (HarperCollins, 1994)
* *The Big Tree* by Bruce Hiscock (Atheneum, 1991)
* *Have You Seen Trees?* by Joanne Oppenheim (Scholastic, 1995)
* *Trees* by Harry Behn (Henry Holt, 1995)

Volunteers Helps children recognize the importance of volunteers to many sectors of our society.

Fiction
* *City Green* by DyAnne DiSalvo-Ryan (William Morrow, 1994)
* *A Symphony of Whales* by Peter Schuch (Harcourt Brace, 1999)
* *Wilfred Gordon McDonald Partridge* by Mem Fox (Kane/Miller, 1984)

Non-Fiction
* *Earth Day* by Linda Lowery (Carolrhoda, 1991)
* *The President Builds a House* by Tom Shachtman (Simon & Schuster, 1989)
* *Up River* by Frank Asch (Simon & Schuster, 1995)

We Celebrate Explores the different cultural traditions that define American society.

Non-Fiction
* *A Carp for Kimiko* by Kathleen Kroll (Charlesbridge, 1993)
* *Happy New Year!* by Emery Bernhard (Lodestar, 1996)
* *Puerto Rico* by Elaine Landau (Children's Press, 1999)

We Vote Explains how voting works and how people use their votes in various situations.

Fiction
* *Amelia Bedelia 4 Mayor* by P. Parish (Greenwillow, 1999)
* *The Ballot Box Battle* by Emily Arnold McCully (Alfred A. Knopf, 1996)
* *Squirrel Park* by Lisa Campbell Ernst (Simon & Schuster, 1993)

Non-Fiction
* *Voting and Elections* by D. Fradin (Children's Press, 1985)
* *Election Day* by Mary Phelan (HarperCollins, 1967)

Photo Credits

Introduction

Cover: Mike Mazzaschi/Stock, Boston/PictureQuest; Title Page: Gary Randall/FPG; Page 3: (top) David Young-Wolff/PhotoEdit, (bottom) Lester Lefkowitz/The Stock Market; Page 5: David Young-Wolff/PhotoEdit/PictureQuest; Page 7: Ken Lax/Bruce Coleman Inc; Page 8: (top left) Jason Hawkes/Stone, (top right) illustration by Tom Leonard, (bottom left) David Young-Wolff/PhotoEdit, (bottom right) Mark Richards/PhotoEdit/PictureQuest; Page 9: (top) D. P. Hershkowitz, (center left, inset) Michael T. Sedam/Corbis, Jim Steinberg/Photo Researchers, (center right) Josh Mitchell/Stone; (bottom left, inset) David R. Frazier/Photo Researchers, Gary Randall/FPG, (bottom right) Chuck Pefley/Stone; Page 10: (top left) David Young-Wolff/PhotoEdit/PictureQuest, (top right) Tom Prettyman/PhotoEdit, (bottom left) David J. Sams/Stone, (bottom right) AP/Wide World Photos; Page 11: (top left) David Lees/Corbis, (top right) David Lees/Corbis, (center left) Dewitt Jones/Corbis, (center right) Gary Braasch/PictureQuest (bottom) Kevin Fleming/Corbis; Page 12: (top) Kim Heacox/Stone, (bottom, first row, left to right) Macduff Everton/Corbis, Kunio Owaki/The Stock Market, David W. Hamilton/The Image Bank, William Johnson/Stock Boston/ PictureQuest, (center row, left to right) Lester Lefkowitz/The Stock Market, Wes Thompson/The Stock Market, Jeff Zaruba/Stone, Chuck Keeler/Stone, (bottom row, left to right) Mike Mazzaschi/Stock Boston/PictureQuest, Alan Schein/The Stock Market, Telegraph Colour Library/FPG, Richard T. Nowitz/Corbis; Page 13: (first row, left half, left to right) David Barnes/The Stock Market, O.S.F./Animals Animals; (second row, right half, top to bottom) Kelly Borsheim/Lumina Candles & Art, Charles D. Winters/Photo Researchers; (second row, top to bottom) The Granger Collection, Northwind Pictures, The Granger Collection, The Granger Collection, Donald C. Johnson/The Stock Market; (third row) Bill Bachmann/Photo Network/PictureQuest; Page 14: Jeff Zaruba/Stone; Page 15: John Running/Black Star/PictureQuest; Page 16: Will & Deni McIntyre/Photo Researchers; Page 17: Phil Schermeister/Corbis; Page 18: Jim Pickerell/Stock Connection; Page 19: Macduff Everton/ Corbis, Kunio Owaki/The Stock Market; Page 21: Gerd Ludwig/Woodfin Camp & Associates

Teacher's Notes

A City Grows: Cover: Mark Segal/Stone; Page 2: Donald C. Johnson/The Stock Market; Pages 2-3: The Granger Collection; Pages 6-7: Northwind Pictures; Page 7: The Granger Collection; Page 16: (from top to bottom) The Granger Collection, Northwind Pictures, The Granger Collection, The Granger Collection, Donald C. Johnson/The Stock Market; *Coming to America*: Cover: The Granger Collection; Page 2: Kevin Fleming/Corbis; Pages 4-5: AP/Wide World Photos; *Communities*: Cover: Jim Pickerell/Stock Connection; Title Page: Lester Lefkowitz/The Stock Market; Page 8: Jeff Zaruba/Stone; Page 16: Bob Daemmrich/Stock Boston/ PictureQuest; *Going West*: Cover: The Everett Collection; Pages 4-5: Culver Pictures; Page 16: The Granger Collection; *Good Neighbors*: Cover: (left) Kevin Miller/Stone, (right) Charles & Josette Lenars/Corbis; Title Page: George Hall/Corbis; *How Paper Is Made*: Cover: Mitch Kezar/Stone; Title Page: Paul Almasy/Corbis; Page 5: Macduff Everton/Corbis; *Keeping Bees*: Cover: Stephen Dalton/Photo Researchers; Page 2: David J. Sams/Stone; Page 3: David Barnes/The Stock Market; Page 6: Andy Sacks/Stone; *Landforms*: Cover: DigitalVision/PictureQuest; Pages 2-3: Frozen Images/The Image Works; Page 5: Wiley/Wales/Index Stock Imagery; *Looking at Money*: Cover: Gail Shumway/FPG; Page 3: illustration by Tom Leonard; Page 7: Corbis, (insets) illustrations by Tom Leonard; Page 16: Laura Dwight/PhotoEdit; *Making Choices*: Cover: Tim Davis/Stone; Title Page: Kevin Fleming/Corbis; Page 7: (top) Ken Karp, (bottom) Elizabeth Crews/Stock, Boston/ PictureQuest; Page 16: Cydney Conger/Corbis; *Maybe I Could*: Cover: Steven W. Jones/FPG; Page 2: Trudi Unger/The Stock Market;